FRONT
OF THE
HOUSE

FRONT
OF THE
HOUSE

Restaurant Manners,
Misbehaviors and Secrets

JEFF BENJAMIN

WITH

GREG JONES

ILLUSTRATIONS BY ROBERT NEUBECKER

BLP

BROOKLINE PUBLIC LIBRARY

647.95
Benjamin
2015

3 1712 01499 1494

Front of the House: Restaurant Manners, Misbehaviors & Secrets
Jeff Benjamin with Greg Jones

Copyright © 2015 by Jeff Benjamin
All rights reserved. No part of this book may be used or reproduced in any form or by any means without written permission, except in the case of reprints for review.

BLP
BURGESS LEA PRESS
NEW HOPE, PENNSYLVANIA

www.burgessleapress.com

1 2 3 4 5 6 7 8 9 10
Printed in the United States of America

Distributed in the United States by Simon & Schuster
Distributed in Canada by Simon & Schuster

Illustrations by Robert Neubecker
Interior design by Alicia Freile
Art direction by Ken Newbaker
Cover design by Whitney Cookman

ISBN: 978-1-941868-02-7
Library of Congress Control Number on file with the publisher

Burgess Lea Press donates 100 percent of our after-tax profits on each book to culinary education, feeding the hungry, farmland preservation and other food-related causes.

Table of Contents

FOREWORD 11

INTRODUCTION

An Iowa Kid in a Clip-on Bow Tie...14
I will always give you cookies

PART ONE: GOING OUT TO DINNER

Word of Mouth 22
Things are not always what they seem

The Art of the Reservation 23
Setting your place at the table

Social Media (Or, Virtually Mad) 29
*"I'm a food blogger, and tomorrow morning the whole world is going
to know that I asked you for something and you didn't give it to me."*

PART TWO: THE RESTAURANT

Designing for Dining 36
A Philadelphia brownstone with soul

Creating Flow 39
*"Running a restaurant is like trying to change
the tires on a car you're driving"*

What's in a Menu? 43
This ain't no South Philly red-sauce joint

PART THREE: AT YOUR SERVICE

Who Taught You That? 48
I take my hospitality lessons when I see them

I Hate Onions! 53
Genuine interest in each guest is the only way to go

Technophobia 56
Put down your phone and pick up the fork

We Take the Blame 59
The customer is always right. Until they're wrong

Help Us Help You 64
Once we start touching them, they're ours

How We Met the Capolinos 67
You've heard of repeat guests? I'm talking hundreds of times

What's Old Is New Again 69
Trends come and go, but farm to table should not be a passing fad

PART FOUR: THE STAFF

Welcome to the Family 76
An employer is more than just the guy who signs the paycheck

Cast of Characters 81
The chef is the quarterback. But let's not forget the dish staff, shall we?

The Hospitality Gene 86
Great waiters are born, not made

The Tipping Point 94
When one server is successful, we're all achievers

Inside the Staff Meeting 97
We're all in this together. So let's eat!

Eight Things Servers Should Know 102
Freshen up, don't pass the buck and learn where to draw the line

PART FIVE: BE OUR GUESTS

One Size Does Not Fit All 106
Every first-time diner is a potential future regular

The Educator 109
"I see four empty tables. Why can't we just sit there? Or there?"

Don't Let Them Get Your Goat 115
Sometimes a disgruntled customer just needs closure

Guests These Days 118
Ma'am, is that a wineglass in your handbag?

Eight Ways to Be a Desirable Customer 124
Show up, do unto others and don't steal the Sweet & Low

PART SIX: DAYS OF WINE

No Merlot! 128
How an independent film turned our wine service upside down

The Amateur Expert 130
"Since I know how much these bottles cost, I simply cannot see myself paying list price"

The Price of Wine 134
It's a lot more than just math

The Price of Corkage 140
Setting standards for the pop-your-own-cork crowd

PART SEVEN: PUTTING SYSTEMS IN PLACE

Greeting and Seating 146
You don't have to see how the sausage is made to enjoy it

The Bar 150
It's not just about alcohol sales

Taking Orders 152
How does she remember what everyone ordered without writing it down?

Checking In...156
We're just bit players in the evening's performance. The guest is the star

Complaints and Comps 160
"You call this medium rare?"

Turning Tables...165
Restaurateurs are just realtors who serve food

Eight Things You May Not Know—But Should 170
Size matters, we don't make the laws and the plate costs more than the food

PART EIGHT: COME AGAIN

One More Cup of Coffee 174
We only get one chance to make a final impression

Speaking of Gratuities...175
Is that how little respect you have for the hospitality industry?

Comment Cards 179
Online feedback and playing the Yelp card

Food Critics..183
Everyone's a critic, but just a few are pros

AFTERWORD 193

ACKNOWLEDGMENTS 199

Foreword

by Marc Vetri

IN CHINESE PHILOSOPHY, the concept of yin-yang explains how opposite or contrary forces are actually complementary—even interconnected. Dark and light, fire and water, sun and moon are all examples of this perfect synergy. I would like to offer one more: Jeff and Marc.

Jeff certainly wasn't the restaurant manager I was looking for. When I was ready to open my first restaurant, Vetri, I had my heart set on some debonair guy from Italy with a cool accent, that endearing way of speaking where there's just enough broken English to make people smile. I was hoping a guy named Roberto from Bergamo would take the job, because he was perfect…or so I thought. I believed Roberto would move to Philadelphia, but after a couple of months of maybes he finally said no.

I was a few short months from opening, and had just signed the lease at 1312 Spruce Street when my brother called and asked, "You know that guy, Jeff Benjamin? The one who works at Restaurant Associates?"

"Of course," I replied.

"Well, he would love to be the manager of your new restaurant."

Really? I thought. *That guy?*

"I don't know," I said to my brother. "He doesn't seem like such a good fit."

"Just throwing it out there, Marc."

"Well, I'll talk to him, but I doubt it'll work out…"

At this point I had known Jeff for a couple of years. Occasionally he would bring dates into Bella Blu, a restaurant at Lexington and 70th in Manhattan where I was the chef before I moved back home

11

to Philly. He was a nice guy, but I just didn't see the front-of-house presence I was looking for. He was certainly no Roberto.

Our meeting went well enough. We talked about wine, which Jeff didn't know much about. We talked about service, which he had only really done for corporate dining. We talked about wardrobe; he owned about thirty blue suits, thirty white shirts and only dark ties. The meeting ended with me saying, "Well, I'll let you know in a week or so." I then spent the next week frantically calling all over Italy trying to convince someone to come manage my new restaurant on Spruce Street. Eventually, left with no alternative, I had to call Jeff. This phone call, unbeknownst to me then, would be the single most important decision of my life.

"Hi Jeff, listen, I don't know if this is gonna work, but I've really got no one else. I'll give you 500 bucks a week, you'll make some tips and if we make any money, I'll give you 25 percent of it."

Looking back at it now, I'm still shocked that he accepted, and two weeks later he moved to Philly. Now after sixteen years, seven restaurants, a charitable foundation, countless research trips to Italy and innumerable hours fine-tuning our craft, we are still the longest relationship either of us has ever had.

A business partnership like ours is not the norm. The staff jokes about us all the time. I turn the volume up on the music at the restaurants, he turns it down. I turn the AC down, he turns it up. On a summer day when I'm in shorts and a T-shirt you'd be hard-pressed to find him in anything other than a suit and tie. (To his credit, he has graduated to lavender shirts and bright ties these days.) We read each other's minds and finish each other's sentences daily. I like to say that with my foot on the gas and his on the brakes, we slowly get to where we want and need to go. He is, for sure, the yin to my yang.

Our relationship works because we trust each other implicitly to make the right decisions, based on what we both believe to be the single most important word in the restaurant industry. I'm not talking about food, or ambiance, or design of the restaurant or even money; I'm talking about hospitality. Not just the hospitality extended to our guests, but to our staff. Jeff and I may come at things from different angles, but our goal is always the same, and it's very simple. We want to make people happy.

If this book you're holding were a manual about standard operations management for the restaurant industry, it would probably be laughed out of the room, because Jeff's lessons are not based entirely on achieving the correct profit margins or conventional business decisions for a restaurant.

They are based on what works for the greater good. They are about building great teams and empowering leaders to take charge. They are based on what he sees as the right fit for each restaurant. Whether he's talking about service, guest relations, staffing, social media, healthcare or employee benefits, there are so many thoughtful, powerful lessons here. When I read this book I was reminded of the decisions made in our early years together and how they were so contrary to popular opinion—yet for some reason, we couldn't fathom doing it any other way.

This book is a real-life look into the actual workings of the restaurant world, but any lesson in it may be extrapolated to other industries. It is a must-read for any cook or front-of-house person, and for anyone who wants to be successful in business. Jeff teaches you to question conventional wisdom and think about how your decisions affect other people.

I shudder to think what my life would be like if Roberto had said yes. Sometimes you just get lucky and the right decision is made for you before you make the wrong one. If that holds true, I'm the luckiest guy in the world.

AN IOWA KID IN A CLIP-ON BOW TIE

I will always give you cookies

NECESSITY IS THE mother of invention, right? Well, in my case it was the mother of my career. There was no grand event that propelled me into the hospitality business. I wasn't born into it. Nothing like that. We moved, that's all.

Being the new kid in a new town at age sixteen, I needed something to do on weekends so that my parents would stop nagging me to study. I did the easiest thing available to me at that time and place—I got a job at a catering hall.

Day one, I donned the requisite black pants, clip-on bow tie and maroon blazer before being introduced to my new boss, Ira. A tall, thin sixty-year-old hippie with curly hair and the thickest Brooklyn accent I ever heard, Ira will forever be the reason I do what I do, thirty years later.

After introductions, he bombarded me with questions: "Have you ever set a table? Can you French serve? Can you flambé bananas at table side?"

"No, no and no."

"No" was my reply to pretty much everything he asked. Never wavering, Ira quickly showed me the ropes of my first double shift—one of hundreds of doubles I'd work there over the course of the next year. As formally attired guests arrived in shiny limos, I had an overwhelming feeling that it was opening night of a grand performance. It was a long day—two hectic five-hour parties with setup and break down in between. Right out of the gate I found myself waiting on dozens of thirteen-year-old bar mitzvah attendees, some trying to sneak booze from the bar, and what's worse, their parents demanded we let them do it! The second party was a wedding reception filled with twenty-somethings who also tried to steal the booze. Through the mayhem, demands and commands were shouted at me from every direction. The frenzied pace and loud live music were dizzying. I loved every minute of it and couldn't wait for more.

To this day, during every preshift meeting, I feel like I'm motivating the cast of a grand show to give it their all for the audience. And it was on that night in September 1985 that I began this run. Well, technically, it was the next morning. At 2:00 a.m., I left Dornstein Catering and headed home to worried parents, announcing on my arrival, "I know what I'm going to do for a living."

More than a decade later Marc Vetri would ask if I'd open a restaurant with him. By then I had gained years of experience in executive dining, where steps of service was my biggest focus. My motivating force was always searching for the best ways to make our guests come back, and Marc recognized that. At the same time that he was wowing our guests with his chicken liver crostini and smoked capon cannelloni, I was demonstrating that I could consistently thread the needle on my side of the kitchen door.

It is on "my" side that I still hang my hat. Sure, the back of the house can cook their butts off; we couldn't work with them if we didn't believe in their product. But we in the front of the house are the conduit between what they do and the guests who are there to enjoy it. It is on our side of the kitchen door that the restaurant makes it or breaks it. There's a lot of good food out there. How it gets to the table and the experience surrounding it—*that's* the delineator. And that's why I do what I do. It's a reality of this business that I understood early on and have embraced ever since. I've held jobs from busboy to runner to server, and even worked as a cook for a spell. I loved them all.

One of my early-career server jobs was at a private country club on Long Island's North Shore. To say the club was exclusive would be a slight understatement. To say this was a wealthy community would be a gross understatement. Having moved east from a small Midwestern town, I'd never experienced such a rarefied atmosphere. The club was in Roslyn Harbor. Each day I'd drive my mom's Oldsmobile Omega to the employee parking lot, walk through the member lot filled with BMWs and Mercedes and head to the employee locker room to change into my tuxedo for the day's service.

All summer long I worked lunch in the mixed grill, a typical country-club dining room. There was also a men-only grill staffed exclusively by female servers. After lunch, I'd take a quick break, wash up and change for dinner service in the main formal dining room. Because it was a limited-membership club, I would be waiting on the same people to whom I had served lunch five hours earlier. Naturally, I got to know them, and they treated me extremely well. I guess there's a don't-bite-the-hand-that-feeds-you mentality in such clubs that goes both ways—if you see the same guests every day, then the guests are seeing the same service staff every day. At minimum, you'd better be cordial to each other. I was the link between what they wanted and what they got, and their satisfaction directly related to my job security.

Every Friday there was a lobster boil. It was crazy. Just about every member came and chowed down on lobster and corn for several frenzied hours. At the end of the meal, we were to deliver a cookie plate to every table. It was a carefully orchestrated production—finish clearing the savory course, crumb the table, deliver cookies. Pretty easy, right? Except that right from the start, Mrs. Schwartz, an older grandmotherly type, would stop me the minute I finished clearing and say, "Now we do get cookies, right?"

"Of course, Mrs. Schwartz, I'll be right back with them."

I'd enter the kitchen, grab the plate and before I could deliver the goods a coworker would invariably appear and say, "Hey, Mrs. Schwartz just stopped me to ask if you forgot her cookies."

Several Fridays passed, and we went through the same exercise every time. I couldn't for the life of me figure out the reason for her impatience. Had she been screwed out of the cookies last summer? Had an employee forgotten to deliver the cookies too many times? She continued to request me as her server, but also to insinuate that I was forgetting her cookies!

I vowed to make it right. Each week, I changed my technique to minimize the ratio of clearing time to cookie delivery, until it got to the point where shortly before removing the savory course I'd store a plate of cookies by the service station, clear the table and immediately run the cookies. But it was still not fast enough to avoid the inevitable query, "Excuse me, Jeffrey, are we getting cookies tonight?"

It became my goal to have this woman full of cookies before she could utter a word. It went like this all summer. In late August, I informed the club manager I would be leaving for college in two weeks. My final night happened to be a Friday, so I had one last chance to make good on my goal. It was an uneventful night and the service-staff-to-guest ratio was low. Before Mrs. Schwartz's table finished their meal, the dining room manager decided to cut half the service staff in order to lower the payroll. Since I had worked lunch and was dangerously close to earning overtime pay, I was the first cut. I walked into the kitchen, said goodbye to my coworkers and hopped into the Omega.

I spent the ride home thinking about the summer, how much money I had made and the car I was going to buy with it. As I drove, happy and hopeful, my mood took a sharp nosedive with the sudden realization: "Mrs. Schwartz never got her cookies!"

This was several years before cell phones, so I sped home, ran into the house and dialed the kitchen line, hoping that someone would answer.

"Hey, is Richie there, this is Jeff Benjamin."

"Yeah, hang on," said the annoyed cook.

A few moments later Richie, the manager, picked up. "What?"

"Richie, I forgot Mrs. Schwartz's cookies!"

There was a long pause… and then all I heard was laughter.

"Are you insane, Benjamin? She gonna starve to death or something? Do you think she didn't ask a million people for her cookies already? For years she's been harassing our staff about the cookie plate. You're the first one to ever give a damn. You've set a pretty bad precedent. Now she's gonna think everyone we hire is as good as you! Have a great time at college, and don't worry about the damn cookies."

To this day, at the end of a service, I do a mental check. Did everyone get the promised experience? Did Mrs. Schwartz get her cookies?

PART ONE

GOING OUT TO DINNER

That personal level of service helps us not only attract diners to our place, but also create regulars

Word of Mouth

Things are not always what they seem

SHORTLY AFTER WE opened Vetri, I was sitting and talking with Marc's dad, Sal. Young at heart but definitely old school, Sal has a perspective on the world that's shared by many in the South Philly neighborhood where he was born and bred. One of my favorite things about Sal is that he's a people person, as well as a real character.

Considering Sal's background and personality, it's no surprise that he had a preconceived notion of what a restaurant should be. More specifically, what an *Italian* restaurant should be. In 1998, most Philadelphians couldn't imagine an Italian restaurant that didn't serve baked ziti or pencil points in red gravy. They didn't know from à la carte. We always joked that we knew when a group had been sent by Sal when they all ordered the same dish—lamb chops—because it came with a vegetable.

So I'm sitting there with Sal, and he says, "Hey Jeff, I got a new place I'm going to take you on your day off."

"Great, Sal. Where is it?" As if I didn't know.

"It's in South Philly, near the other place I took you."

"What's it like?"

"Italian."

"But what makes it different?"

"Well, I took my friend Bobby there the other night and it was tremendous."

"Oh? What did you have?"

"I had a swordfish steak. It came with pasta and a salad. Bobby had veal. And they didn't give him no trouble when he asked for a vegetable instead of pasta. It was great!"

"But how *was* it, Sal?"

"Big! The fish didn't even fit on the plate!"

"But how'd it *taste*?"

"Oh, it was okay."

If you're going to ask for a recommendation, consider the source. A great recommendation isn't worth a hill of beans if it isn't relevant to the way you dine out. Our customers at Vetri come to us because we offer them something special that they can't get anywhere else in Philadelphia.

Marc and I are fortunate to be in a business that will never fall victim to e-commerce. You will always need to come to us; you can't have a "virtual" Vetri meal. There is no way to enjoy our work without sitting in our dining room, reading the wine list, soaking in the atmosphere and appreciating the service. I love that about the restaurant business; it's what led me here and keeps me here.

But when it comes to how people pick a place to eat, that's a different story. This is one area where technology, for better or worse, has permeated the hospitality industry. I still believe that asking a friend for a recommendation is really the best method. Just consider the way it used to be.

Back in '98, there was no social media—Mark Zuckerberg hadn't had his bar mitzvah yet, and the Vetri Family didn't even have a marketing budget. We relied on word of mouth. Every guest became part of our de facto marketing department, and we knew that we had to give them a product they felt good about selling. There was no magic wand, no clever tweet, no viral video that would compel a new guest to call and say, "Hey, do you have room for two tonight?"

Around the turn of the last century, the ultimate source for restaurant recommendations was Tim and Nina Zagat—the Zagats plus thousands of their "friends." The story goes that Tim and Nina, lawyers who had settled in New York City, dined out frequently and constantly solicited restaurant advice from friends and colleagues. They kept copious notes and soon found others asking them for "the list." What started as a hobby eventually became a published guide. It first covered just New York City but grew into a successful enterprise. To fill such comprehensive guides, the Zagats expanded their circle of reviewers beyond friends and family—it was basically word-of-mouth in written form. To this day, even with abundant internet competition, I believe Zagat remains one of the most reputable sources for dining advice.

On the other hand, things are not always as they seem.

For years, we saw an influx of reservation requests directly attributable to Zagat. People used it as their dining bible. How it worked so effectively was beyond me, as I could never get around the obvious questions: Were those reviewers vetted? Were they experts? Were they sincere? Who knows? But one thing we do know is that it worked so well, certain people took advantage. Consider this exchange, which was not uncommon during the height of Zagat's popularity:

"Hi, I'd like a reservation for four on Saturday night."

"Of course, sir, let me check the availability. It looks like I can accommodate you at nine o'clock."

"Oh, no. I was looking for something closer to seven."

"Certainly, I'm happy to keep an eye out for that time slot. However, currently those tables are reserved."

"I'm a Zagat reviewer, you know."

Pause.

First, anyone who wanted to be an unpaid Zagat reviewer could be—simply eat at a restaurant, write some notes and send them off to Tim and Nina. Second, a professional food critic would never announce themselves in order to get preferential treatment and would know better than to expect a table to magically appear in a popular thirty-five-seat restaurant at seven o'clock on a Saturday night.

"Of course, sir, and we'd be delighted to have you. I will continue to monitor the waitlist until Saturday."

More often than not, we were able to accommodate Mr. and Mrs. "Reviewer." Not because we thought they'd send comments to Zagat, but because filling seats is what we do.

We also knew that, whether or not they filed a review with Zagat, they would certainly file it with their friends.

The same holds true today. And whether someone spreads the word by phone, email, tweet, text or in person, as long as we give them the right promotional materials—a delicious meal, memorable atmosphere and singular service—we like our chances of getting their recommendation.

The Art of the Reservation

Setting your place at the table

IN 2000, VETRI HAD BEEN open for two years. We had enjoyed a wildly successful debut, with critics and customers alike embracing our innovative style of dining. Marc was serving regional Italian dishes like spit-roasted baby goat with soft polenta and sweetbread ravioli with braised veal sauce, and I was steadily growing our wine list. We were collecting accolades and regulars at a brisk clip.

Despite that early success, we still had a grand total of just eight employees, two of whom were Marc and me. In addition to the sexier responsibilities like creating an intriguing menu and curating an impressive wine collection, the two of us answered the phones and wrote reservations in a notebook daily. We spoke to every guest long before they sat at our table, and we knew the value of that interaction.

Before the technology revolution, excelling in a restaurant was all about a well-earned reputation on both sides of the kitchen door. We were always on our toes. I'd hear the phone ring and bound from the dining room to our office—at that time a closet in the basement—to answer the phone as if I'd been waiting all day for that call. If it rang more than three times, we considered it a failure. Forget about putting someone on hold to deal with another crisis. We didn't have a hold button! Since every call was so precious, we asked questions and took copious notes. "Have you been here before? Is there a special occasion? Do you have a table preference? Yes, we can accommodate you." That last line was always the most important. Before you'd sampled one bite of our food, or even seen a menu, you knew how we felt about you.

Today you just pick up your electronic device and make a reservation with a few clicks. You don't have to talk to anyone in order to secure your place at the table. Great, right?

Don't get me wrong: I love technology. I love efficiency even more. If I can cut down on the amount of time it takes to perform a task to our high standards, I'm all for it. And since our sole purpose is to provide guest service, if the guest wants the option to book a reservation online for the sake of convenience, then it's a service we know we should—and do—provide. Even if we did enter the technology game kicking and screaming.

Back in 2000, a local rep for a brand-new website knocked on Vetri's door.

"Hi, I represent a company called Open Table. Our website was designed to help maximize your reservations and save labor dollars at the same time," Joe said, standing in the doorway.

As half of the team that personally took every reservation, I was skeptical of what Joe was peddling. As for the promise of saving labor dollars, I wasn't quite in that arena yet.

"Okay, tell me how it works," I said reluctantly.

"It's simple. Your restaurant buys a license to use our software, you upload your floor plan layout and menu, and you maintain regular access to our website. When a guest wants to make a reservation at Vetri, they go to opentable.com, type in Vetri, select an available time and they have a reservation. Best of all, you no longer have to pay a reservationist! You can build a database with notes about the guests, so next time they come you will know how many times they've been in, their food and drink preferences and any other info you want to add. It's a great tool. Everyone's going to be doing it!"

It's ironic that I didn't immediately jump on board, considering the conversation Marc and I had had just a month before Joe's visit.

"Hey Jeff, I've been thinking," he said one morning while we were sitting at the desk we shared for eight years. "Maybe we should have a website or email account or something. What do you think?"

"Hmm. Isn't that expensive? How much does a website cost? Can't we just give our personal email accounts to people to contact us?"

"Yeah, but wouldn't it be cool if you could just log on and see our menu and stuff? Maybe even make reservations directly on the website?"

"I think it might be neat, but are people really going to websites to pick restaurants and make reservations?"

"I think they may at some point," Marc said. "I'm going to look into it."

Back to Joe from Open Table.

"When do I actually talk to the guest?" I asked him.

"When they arrive! You don't need to have any interaction with them at all. They get an email the day before as a reminder, and if they need to change the reservation they just go online and do it themselves. You never have to talk to the guest at all. It's beautiful!"

"So let me get this straight. I'm in the business of guest interaction—I do what I do because I love people. I enjoy meeting them, I celebrate their differences and I take pleasure in bringing them joy. And now you're saying I don't *have to* interact with them?"

The look on my face told Joe he wouldn't be making a sale that day. "You see, there's a total disconnect between what you do and what I do. The way I see it, I *get to* talk to the guest. It's my privilege," I explained.

Then I thanked Joe and escorted him out.

Fortunately, he was persistent, and we continued to speak over the next few months. He was interested in hearing my perspective and eventually convinced me to come onboard by suggesting a unique angle on using the service: I could block all reservation slots on the site—effectively rendering the system useless for booking tables—while using the system to enter reservations we had taken ourselves, as well as guest notes. That last part was the part I loved, the tool that helped me learn more about my guests.

Over time, we realized it was essential to allow patrons in the digital age the opportunity to book online directly, and now full-service Internet reservations are available at our restaurants. I do admit this has maximized seating capacity and allowed us to more fully book less-desirable times. However, I have been cautious about how much labor cost Open Table saves us, if any, since we use online reservations as a tool to enhance the experience, not as a complete replacement for personal interaction.

Every guest who makes an online reservation at Vetri receives a phone call within the hour to confirm the date, welcome them and let them know how excited we are that they're coming. We have taken an otherwise impersonal internet tool and used it to make the guest interaction even more pronounced. It isn't feasible to do this in all of our restaurants, which record thousands of reservations a month. But whenever possible, if a guest has made a note or special request as part of their online reservation, we use that as a moment to start the interaction.

Now more than ever, it is imperative that we remember our values and principles and keep in mind why we do what we do. The minute you consider sacrificing integrity for a shortcut that fundamentally alters your business model, maybe the better solution is to do something else, or modify the shortcut to create something closer to your core. That personal level of service helps us not only get customers but also create regulars.

And while we're on the subject of the power of the telephone, on more than one occasion a simple phone call has led to a lifelong friendship.

One morning, years ago, Marc ran to the basement to answer the phone. "Hello, Vetri. How may I help you?"

The voice said, "I'm hoping to dine at your place tonight. Can you accommodate me?"

Back then, our weeknights were not very busy, but weekends were packed, and we did just two turns on Fridays and Saturdays. This particular call came on a Saturday.

"Sir, I wish we could," Marc replied, "but tonight we're fully committed. I'm happy to take your name and number and contact you if we have a cancellation. Or maybe you can come Monday?"

"Oh, no. I'm only here for one night. I was at DiBruno's this afternoon and asked if they supplied any restaurants who bought solely based on quality, not price. Without missing a beat they said, 'Vetri.' So I thought I'd give it a shot."

"I'm so sorry we'll miss you. Do you get to Philadelphia often? Maybe you can come in next time?"

"Two or three times a year, tops. I'm in from Iowa."

"My partner, Jeff, is from Iowa! How many people are you hoping to dine with tonight?"

"It's just me. I'm very flexible on time, and will even stand in the kitchen!"

"You will? Why don't you come in around eight-thirty, nine o'clock? You can hang out in the kitchen, and at some point we'll get you a table."

"That's great! I'll be there."

That night, the guy entered the restaurant with the biggest smile on his face and walked right up to me.

"You're Jeff?" he asked, then introduced himself. "I hear you're from Fairfield."

I soon found him a seat, and throughout the night we maintained an ongoing dialogue as if I was his de facto dining partner. We had a lot of things in common, and even our one major difference—I'm a Cubs fan and he's for the Cardinals—produced an entertaining exchange that continues to this day.

Since that night, he's returned to Vetri every time he's visited Philly. He has attended my kids' birthday parties, shared family time with us and we even took a business trip to Italy when he opened a food-importing business. From one simple phone call, a lifelong friendship was forged.

Hey Joe, can a computer do that?

Social Media (Or, Virtually Mad)

"I'm a food blogger, and tomorrow morning the whole world is going to know that I asked you for something and you didn't give it to me"

WHEN I WAS IN COLLEGE, a certain TV commercial for shampoo starring Heather Locklear made a lasting impression.

Heather's line was: "It was so good that I told two friends about it, and they told two friends and so on and so on and so on."

Each time she added another "and so on" her bright blonde image duplicated until there were dozens of Heather Locklears onscreen. For me, it's an indelible visual of how a favorable personal review can spread.

Anyone who studied business in college will remember this old rule of thumb: "If a customer has a good experience with a product or service, they *may* tell a friend. But if a customer has a bad experience, they *will* tell thirty friends."

With the Internet, the concept of word-of-mouth reviews got turned on its ear. By the time Yelp took hold in 2004, telling thirty friends about your bad experience over the course of a couple weeks had transmogrified into telling thirty thousand strangers over the course of several milliseconds. With one click, we now submit our reviews not only to our friends, but also to their friends, and so on and so on and so on.

It used to be that a customer who chose to leave our restaurant unsatisfied simply wouldn't come back. Maybe they'd tell a friend, "Hey, I went there and it didn't live up to the hype." And maybe their friend would say, "Really? I've been there a few times and every time it was great," and convince them to try again. Or worse, the friend might say, "I've never been, though I always heard how great it was. Maybe I shouldn't try it now." And that would be a loss for both of us since we'd never get the chance to prove ourselves.

The problem isn't that everybody with a computer is a food blogger—and believe me, everybody with a computer *is* a food blogger—but rather the way they go about it. Instead of quietly taking notes to pepper your blog post with later, why not talk to us in the moment, explain what you want and within a few moments, receive it? It sounds crazy, but some people really would rather endure a bad experience in silence in order to rage loudly against the restaurant later—SOMETIMES IN ALL CAPS.

On one hand, I sort of get it—who doesn't like to unload a good rant? But on the other hand, I really don't get it—who wouldn't trade a good rant for a great meal any day of the week?

How did this become an acceptable thing to do? Have I ever walked into your office, engaged your services, kept my thoughts to myself and then later posted my review online? If I am paying you for goods or services and you ask for my input—and even if you don't—I guarantee that upon feeling any dissatisfaction I would simply say, "You know, I think you could prepare this case a little bit better," or, "Aren't there other options you can consider to heal my daughter quicker?" I wouldn't zip it in your presence and then later go post online, "As far as lawyers go, this one SUCKS!" or, "That doctor is a bigger quack than Daffy Duck!"

For whatever reason, the hospitality industry in particular has become the target of vitriol across the Internet. Blame it on bad food television shows. And don't get me wrong; I oppose censorship and I appreciate all honest feedback. It's the anonymous lies presented as honest feedback, and the obvious trolling, that I have the biggest problem with.

One thing I love about Open Table is that it encourages diners to return to the site after visiting a restaurant and describe their experience—good or bad—using their real names. We do monitor online reviews from reputable sites, and if we notice trends— multiple comments about a particular dish, or several notes about one server—we take action internally. On very rare occasions, we reply to a commenter directly. In general, it's not a good idea to engage in public exchange with a customer in any online forum; we'd just end up sounding defensive or worse, desperate.

The irony is that we can actually prove when a complaint is not legit. If a guest claims that we "lost the reservation and so they made us wait an extra thirty minutes for a table," we check the system and discover that we did in fact have their reservation correct, but that they showed up on the wrong night or went to the wrong restaurant (no mention that we managed to fit them in anyway). Or if a guest complains that "it took forty minutes after we finished our appetizers to get our entrées," we can check the point-of-service (POS) system and see that the entrées were delivered thirty minutes after the appetizers were ordered, so unless the guest ate their apps in negative-ten minutes, there's no way the complaint was valid. Unfortunately, it's just not worth pointing these things out.

What irks me most is this unlimited ability for anyone to comment however they want, regardless of the complaint's basis in reality. No fact checking. No filter. These are just cyberbullies, not legitimate food critics or diners who care.

Still, I truly do enjoy reading the numerous trustworthy food blogs and websites, just like I used to enjoy reading food magazines when print media was all there was. To me, legitimate food blogs are to quality magazines what illegitimate food blogs are to scribbled rants on a bathroom wall. It's usually easy to tell the difference, too, because the shady bloggers are the ones who pound their chests the most.

"I'm a food blogger, and tomorrow morning the whole world is going to know that I asked you for something and you didn't give it to me." I've heard this threat too many times. One quick Google search would reveal that said food blogger is actually a bank employee by day who has twenty-five followers on his free Wordpress site.

I would be doing social media a disservice if I didn't mention the positives we get from it. One of the greatest things that ever happened to my business, in fact, is the ability to advertise for free online. When used judiciously, Twitter, Facebook, Snapchat and Instagram are wonderful tools, and nothing makes a restaurant happier than when a guest replies to one of our posts in kind. But as a rule, we keep it positive through all of our tweets and chats. I am constantly amazed at the number of business owners and managers who respond negatively to tweets and other online barbs directed their way. We are easy targets, and to respond any other way than positively—with the exception of not responding at all—is something we simply don't do.

I guarantee that if I posted a picture of our best pasta this very second, then checked back an hour later, I'd see at least one comment that goes something like this: "Mama mia! That sauce looks gooier than _____." Fill in the blank with something unsavory, and you've got the picture.

PART TWO

THE
RESTAURANT

*"You know, to really understand what
it is I want to do with Vetri,
you've got to come with me to Italy."*

Designing for Dining

A Philadelphia brownstone with soul

A FEW YEARS AGO, tapas restaurants were all the rage. The combination of flavorful Spanish dishes on small plates designed for sharing with friends was something that Marc and I both really enjoyed. So we talked about opening a tapas place. The conversation lasted just a few minutes.

Ultimately, we admitted what we already knew—that you really can't sit around a table and say, "Hey, let's open a restaurant; what kind should we do? How about tapas?" It would be obvious to most diners that you weren't in it for the right reason, and the lack of authenticity would be painfully apparent. There would be no soul. It may sound a bit esoteric, but it's the truth—a restaurant needs to have soul. Without it, the result is almost certainly soulless food and service.

In the process of opening Vetri, Marc wore his soul on his sleeve. He approached all facets of concept, design and construction with intense attention to detail, and every decision was touched by a particular inspiration. He constantly referenced foods, colors, styles and accessories from his time spent in northern Italy, and although I'd never been at that point, his excitement became my excitement.

The chosen space—a brownstone in the middle of a residential block—had been home to successful restaurants in the past, including Philadelphia's famed Le Bec-Fin. Setting up shop in this particular room was very important to Marc, not so much for practical reasons like location or floor plan, but because it was hallowed ground. It had heart; it had soul.

He spent a great deal of time choosing paint colors. That same love went into picking out linens, chairs, plates, glasses, lighting and— even though we were on a shoestring budget at the time—properly weighty flatware. My years in the executive dining rooms of Wall Street's biggest banks had given me some valuable perspective in these areas, ensuring that Marc's vision worked within the standards of fine dining as well as our budget. When making these choices, in addition to form and function you have to factor in breakage and theft. You can't afford place settings for thirty-five unless you can afford them for three times that number.

Looking through catalogs and showrooms wasn't all we did; we also got down and dirty in the renovation. Marc and I spent the better part of a week on our hands and knees stripping and staining the old hardwood floors, doing our best to match the colors and textures that he recalled from a couple of places in Italy that he admired.

"Wow," I remember thinking. "I left a high-paying corporate job to open a restaurant with this guy who frankly is a bit obsessed. I haven't earned a dollar in over a month and I'm staining floors on my hands and knees trying to match a color from some restaurant in a village in northern Italy."

Still, I couldn't have been happier. I knew the day would come when I'd be walking those floors with a room full of our own guests, welcoming them with pride into the space that we created to enjoy an experience that they simply could not have anywhere else.

Soon after we opened, Marc said to me, "You know, to really understand what it is I want to do with Vetri, you've got to come with me to Italy."

Who'd say no? We hopped on a plane and started making the rounds of Marc's old haunts. The moment I walked into the first restaurant, it all clicked. The color on the wall was the color on the wall of our restaurant! The next restaurant had menus and furnishings that looked like ours. Another place was playing the music that we play, and there were dishes everywhere that were reminiscent of our own. I realized then that what Marc wanted to do with Vetri—in fact, what he had done—was to bring to Philadelphia the passion he had experienced in Lombardia. No amount of market research can duplicate that kind of inspiration.

Of course, once you have your concept down, you have to get into the details. That's the fun part. You stand in the space, walk around the space, get a feel for the space.

"What if we did this over here? And what if we did that over there? How will it *feel* to guests?"

To complement the rich wood tones of the floor, chairs and cabinetry, Marc hired a young (i.e., inexpensive) art student to paint a mural on the wall across from the entrance. And because every dining room needs a focal point, Marc had the inspiration to place a beautiful antique Berkel meat slicer adjacent to the mural. Its addition actually cost the room a couple of seats in terms of space, but in the long run, getting the atmosphere right will contribute more to your success than adding to the head count. The imposing red slicer created a memorable visual moment for each guest who entered, and it became such an important element to the room that we added a Berkel slicer to all of our restaurants.

Years after we opened Vetri, Marc visited the Murano glass factory near Venice. He fell in love with a chandelier and ordered one on the spot, calling me from his hotel to advise me not to put anything on our credit card for a while. It was probably the biggest impulse buy I've ever seen, but it's been well worth it. The chandelier has become the focal point of the room and adds such warmth and elegance that when we finally opened our upstairs dining room at Vetri in 2014, Marc ordered another Murano chandelier.

Of course, not every restaurant needs an expensive chandelier to deliver the desired look and feel. When we started conceiving our gastropub, Alla Spina (Italian for "on tap"), we obviously needed to create an altogether different feel from Vetri, yet no less authentic.

The craft beer scene was already thriving in America when we noticed it taking off in Italy during our frequent visits. The concept hit both of us at the same time; it was an easy, natural decision to open an Italian gastropub. The challenge was to create an environment that blended the popular American scene with influences from Italy.

Once again, Marc and I hit the road. After traveling thousands of miles to gastropubs from Italy to New York City and beyond, we were ready. Since Alla Spina is in an old car dealership in Center City, we knew we wanted the design to honor that history and energy. The choices of poured cement floors and twisted aluminum walls came naturally, but the real inspiration was hiring a graffiti artist to cover the walls with high-impact urban art. All the design elements combined to create a casual, exciting atmosphere. The look of the room captured the Philly part of the equation, but our fact-finding mission had as much to do with the food as it did the design.

We hired an accomplished chef with great beer-scene credentials to run the kitchen. And while we spent a lot of time devising a menu with just the right beer-friendly dishes, like mortadella hot dogs with cabbage relish and fried snails in parsleyed tartar sauce, it seemed we spent a *crazy* amount of time perfecting the French fries. In this scene, a place is only as good as its fries. We experimented with cutting methods, heat levels, cooking times and even resting times. Skin on or skin off? Should we serve the fries right out of the fryer, or let them sit out a couple of minutes? How often should we change the oil? Each of these questions resulted in numerous experiments until we honed the recipe. Now the beef-fat fries at Alla Spina are legendary.

Of course, there really is no final form to any restaurant concept and design. In fact, that original Berkel slicer that inspired us to place one in all of our restaurants is no longer on display at Vetri. Like everything else, restaurants need to change and grow, even if it means retiring the focal point that guests have grown comfortable with. The beauty is that these changes don't happen on any kind of schedule, but rather by feel. And when inspiration hits, it's always wise to follow.

Creating Flow

"Running a restaurant is like trying to change the tires on a car you're driving"

THE NEXT TIME YOU arrive at a restaurant with a group of five and a reservation for four and casually suggest that the server simply add another chair, please know that it really is not as simple as it looks.

This issue pops up frequently. The common "solution" offered by guests is to jam in another chair and place setting. I don't blame them for coming to this conclusion—we've all had family meals at home where the dining room table meant for ten suddenly needs to seat fifteen. You grab a few folding chairs from the basement and everyone crams together happily. The worst that can happen is an accidental elbow to somebody's ribs.

But in a restaurant, accommodating one guest can easily disrupt another. That's why we spend hours on the initial planning of a room, placing furniture and testing the flow. We actually have staff sit in all the chairs and banquettes at adjacent tables, then start moving around as guests do—getting in and out of the seats, leaning back, crossing and uncrossing their legs, sliding a few feet in each direction. It can get pretty comical, and it may sound like overkill, but this exercise actually provides valuable information. It's no surprise that lots of money is spent in the restaurant business to determine logistics that improve efficiency.

We can travel near and far to look for inspiration in design, colors, textures and everything else that goes into setting up a restaurant. We can go to Italy, eat in some great places and engage in fruitful conversations with families who have been serving food for centuries. We can come back and spend weeks searching for the perfect furniture and accessories to fill the room. But at the end of the day, every aesthetic choice has to meet a more important requirement: efficiency.

The restaurant business is a fast-paced, lively work environment. The only way it functions properly is if the staff, their tools and their surroundings are set up for maximum efficiency. My friend Jefferson Macklin, president of Barbara Lynch Gruppo restaurants in Boston, recently commented that running a restaurant is like trying to change the tires on a car you're driving, which perfectly illustrates the challenges of this business.

There's something special about restaurant designers that sets them apart from those who design other workspaces. The best restaurants combine function with aesthetics, and there are many elements to consider. The fact is, every item in the dining room— every chair, table, china cabinet, light and light switch—has been placed where it is for a reason. Nothing about it is simple. Changing one salient detail of a restaurant can negatively affect the flow of the whole room, and all possibilities must be considered before one piece of furniture is placed.

One busy night at Osteria Moorestown, our 120-seat suburban New Jersey restaurant serving Neapolitan and Roman-style pizza and wood-grilled entrées, a fairly large group showed up with a couple of extra guests. Only a few large tables were available, and none were ideal, but we had to accommodate the group. After a few minutes of deliberation, we decided to move the whole table a couple of feet to one side to create enough space for guests at adjacent tables to pass, then added a couple more seats and place settings to an already tight fit. Once things had been rearranged, everyone took their seats, hungry for a good meal.

Everyone, that is, except the guy on the end who ended up directly under a spotlight. This light had been carefully situated to illuminate the area next to the table and provide visibility for guests entering and exiting. But suddenly, it looked as if it had been placed by an interrogator to extract a confession from a prisoner. The server noticed that the poor guy would soon be sweating from the heat, and suggested that he go have a drink at the bar (on us) while someone got a small ladder and figured out a way to divert the light.

Speaking of light, the McDonald's corporation spent hundreds of thousands of dollars to determine that very bright lights and colorful plastic chairs would cause their guests to eat fast and leave fast, thus enabling them to turn their tables more quickly. Although we, too, invest significant time and energy on lighting—both in the planning stages and every night during service—our goal is much different. Like McDonald's, we need to turn our tables, but more than that we need you to be comfortable.

Have you ever noticed the light changing in a restaurant? You really shouldn't, even though we're constantly tinkering with it. Almost every light is equipped with a dimmer, and we spend time before service begins setting each one to its optimum output—bright enough to illuminate the menu and show you where you're going, but not so bright that you feel edgy. All night we monitor the light, and notice when the sun sets, especially in summer when we're well into our second turn before the light fades. Once in a great while, a staff member manning the dimmer will slide the switch too far and cause a jarring blast in someone's eyes. Like a lot of the things that we do in restaurants, guests never notice we're doing them until we mess up ever so slightly.

When it comes to efficiency, we notice everything, from table props like small vases and candles to bottle placement in the bar to equipment placement in the kitchen. While turning tables is crucial, it's just as important that guests never feel rushed. The best way to serve both needs is to tighten up efficiency in all areas.

The table props, for instance, are chosen not just for looks, but for ease of cleaning between courses and between turns. The bottles in the service bar are placed for quick access based on popularity. I've seen restaurant bars that are clearly set up for excitement but take forever to make a drink—and to me, waiting is not exciting.

Our kitchen, too, is arranged so that the most popular foods are prepared closest to the pass where servers pick up plates to be served. If we're serving a lot of pasta, then the boiler shouldn't be way over in a far corner. While these points may sound ridiculously minor taken individually, it's the compound effect we're going for. By paying attention to details that save us eight minutes per turn, we've just gained eight more minutes for every guest to enjoy, while also meeting our business goals.

In the restaurant business, we have to change, grow and stimulate ourselves and our guests. That's why, despite the time we spend getting everything just right, we regularly change the setup in every one of our restaurants.

By "regularly," I don't mean year after year on the first of January. Typically, change is initiated on the spur of the moment, when we're struck with an inspiration. Because that can happen when we least expect it, it's that much more exciting for us and, hopefully, for our guests.

On the other hand, when we feel it's time for a change but the bright idea simply hasn't hit yet, we always have the option to take a vacation—I mean, a business trip—to Italy to seek a meeting with our muse.

What's in a Menu?

This ain't no South Philly red-sauce joint

BEFORE WE OPENED AMIS, our Roman-style neighborhood trattoria, Marc and I spent a week in Italy sampling typical trattoria dishes. We ordered cacio e pepe pasta at every meal, day after day—not because we loved it, but because it would have been foolish to order it once and think, "Okay, we understand this dish. On to the next pasta."

What if on the night we had ordered it the chef was having a bad day? What if we happened to walk into the one restaurant in Rome that didn't serve cacio e pepe in the traditional manner? Comparing several versions of a classical dish is a sound way to understand the dish at its core, and on that trip, as always, we were looking for menu inspiration.

Just as the concept, design and physical setup of the dining room come together through inspiration and hard work, the menu requires great attention to detail. Size, shape, material, font style, descriptive copy, item placement, design and the choice of dishes are all carefully considered. Putting together a menu is labor intensive, but it's driven by fun and passion.

There's no blueprint or checklist. We don't say, "Okay, we need one beef dish, two chicken, five pastas." Instead, it's an ongoing conversation. Our culinary team throws out ideas based on their own travel and hands-on research, study of classic dishes and trends, recipe testing and retesting, seasonal influences and ingredient availability. Gradually, we whittle down the options.

If you're going to open a restaurant inspired by a specific culture or region, you need to really delve into the local food in the type of place you're trying to emulate. When Vetri first opened, presented as an authentic northern Italian ristorante, our menu set off many guests and critics who questioned its contents—both what was there and what wasn't.

Our capretto, or baby goat, which I discuss in detail later, was often targeted as "not Italian food" even though it has been a mainstay in northern Italy for generations.

And to this day, we still field questions about the menu's lack of red sauce and garlic—two ingredients rarely used in northern Italian cuisine but popular in the country's south. It took people a while to realize that we really *were* an authentic Italian restaurant, just not the kind they were used to. Most Italian Americans in Philadelphia trace their roots to southern Italy, and that food has long been the standard in America. It's no different than if a chef from Puglia had taken regular business trips to Dallas for several years and then decided to open an American-style restaurant back home. Odds are, his menu would not include Maine lobster, Maryland crab cakes or Cajun gumbo, but lots of authentic Texas barbecue. And that would be just fine, but not representative of America.

Once the right dishes have been selected for the menu, the rest is all about presentation. A menu's style and design explain what kind of place you are running, and when the menu and milieu don't match, it can be glaring. A fast-casual spot would likely feature cool fonts and text colors, highlighting on certain words, spirited illustrations—or maybe it's handwritten. The menu in a more elegant setting will generally have a much finer script, less flash and more white space.

And what about size? In fine dining, the menu is more reserved and less crowded, so it tends to cover several pages, and that doesn't include the wine list. But our gastropub Alla Spina is more of a bar, so the entire menu fits on one page—we just want you to look it over, choose what you want, get a beer, eat some food and have some fun. At Amis, a step up from Alla Spina, we have bruschetta and appetizers on the left side and entrées on the right, where your eyes are drawn to first. Most people choose their entrée first, then decide on a first course. Much thought goes into all of this, and the key is to make it look uncontrived.

But of course, it is contrived. The restaurant industry has commissioned psychological studies to determine where your eyes go when you pick up a menu, revealing a host of subliminal suggestions that can maximize revenue. Knowing how people approach a menu also helps us make it easier for guests to get the most out of their experience. For example, since we obviously serve pasta, it doesn't have to take up prime location on the top right of page one because we know that you'll search for it. Instead, that prime space can feature our signature dishes, inspired by our travels in Italy. We devote a section on one of our menus to Il Quinto Quarto, or the "fifth quarter," featuring variety meats such as tripe, tongue and sweetbreads. We need to highlight these dishes to let those who enjoy them know that we have them.

When a particular dish isn't selling, we'll consider all factors, including its description on the menu, to figure out the problem. The first step, of course, is to taste a couple of different plates to determine if it's the food that needs to be fixed. If we're satisfied with the presentation and flavors, we'll rethink how it's presented on the menu. At Alla Spina we used to offer Welsh rarebit, but it wasn't selling despite the fact that it was absolutely delicious. Someone suggested changing the name to "beer cheese toast," and now we can't keep it in the kitchen.

The irony of menu development is that, after all the time and effort we spend to get it just right, every so often we change it. While certain mainstay dishes will always be offered, others are swapped in and out due to seasonality, availability of ingredients, the weather and really just change for change's sake. You may not want a heavy ragu in August, for example, but come December such hearty food seems just right. At Pizzeria Vetri, our menu will include margherita pizza every day of the year, but we only add the corn-based pizza in late summer.

The dynamic nature of the menu keeps it interesting not just for guests who visit frequently, but also for everyone in the kitchen. We all love food, but chefs and cooks have a more complex relationship with it. The more they get to experiment and create new dishes, the better for everyone.

PART THREE

AT YOUR SERVICE

*Of course, there are times
when you may think you're going
the extra mile, but in reality you're
going a mile too far.*

Who Taught You That?

I take my hospitality lessons when I see them

MOST PEOPLE KNOW good service when they experience it. Often, however, that awareness doesn't move past the subconscious level. They may sense that something special has transpired, but not comment on it to themselves or their companions. They simply leave with the sensation that this is a business they'll want to do business with again.

Those of us who work in the service industry don't take such instances for granted; we take them to heart. Born with the hospitality gene, we are hyperaware when a situation occurs that calls for one of us to either rise to the occasion or fall flat on our faces. And we take note. If we're good, we learn something.

When I visit my colleagues' restaurants, I'd be a fool not to take note of service methods I can either emulate or use as a teachable moment on what not to do. Learning opportunities are everywhere. My thirst for knowledge is surpassed only by my love of people, and those are the two factors that drive me every day. I'm always intrigued when I see a brilliant hospitality detail in a setting where I least expect it, and I put those lessons to use.

One summer I was driving my family home to Philadelphia after a visit with my mother on Long Island. It was Sunday night and the New Jersey Turnpike near Exit 7 was a mess. Toss in a cranky four-year-old and two-year-old, and that drive had the potential to become unbearable. So before things grew worse, we decided to stop at the Joyce Kilmer service area for a quick bite and diaper change.

We weren't the only ones with that idea—the line was easily ninety deep, including a busload of kids who just beat us to the entrance. While my wife, Melissa, took the kids to the bathroom, I reluctantly joined what I assumed would be the slowest fast-food line ever. If I hadn't moved a sufficient distance before my family returned, we probably would have just left. Then I witnessed an unexpected customer service event I have never forgotten.

As my family walked toward me and Plan B was starting to look inevitable, three employees came around to the front of the stand with pen and paper in hand and started taking orders. By the time I arrived at the register, mere minutes later, they had packaged up my order and we quickly finished the transaction. I couldn't help myself; I had to say something to the nearest staff member.

"Excuse me, I saw what you and your coworkers did by coming around to the front and taking orders to reduce the wait time. Is that standard procedure for your company?"

She hesitated, clearly wondering if this might get her in trouble, and said, "No, I don't think so. I just thought that since we had all finished assembling food, and you all were going to be waiting a long time, we could take orders then run back and continue packing them up. I sure wouldn't want to wait in such a long line!"

This woman wasn't following company protocol by encouraging her teammates to step up; she was performing genuine hospitality. "That is incredible," I said. "I'm so glad you did that for us. Thank you."

I thought of her again the following week during a busy Friday night at Osteria. Moving through the restaurant, I noticed that the bar had gotten at least three deep with guests waiting for their tables. Those seated at the bar had all been served, and the first row of standers was ordering, but those in the back were caught in a frustrating limbo without a table or a drink. I suggested to the service bartender that he walk around to the third row of people and quickly take drink orders before getting back to handle his next ticket. In minutes, guests who had been miserably waiting were happily sipping. It is now standard practice in our restaurants to perform this relatively casual act of customer service.

On the opposite end of the spectrum from fast-food rest stops is the Four Seasons hotel chain. When it comes to first-class accommodations, most travelers would agree that Four Seasons sets a certain standard. But it is in the space where you would least expect family-friendly service that I've had the most valuable takeaways from them.

In the early days of our company, I wasn't your typical Four

Seasons guest. I had a growing family and travel budgetary constraints. My wife, kids and I were heading to Chicago to visit friends and to see my beloved Cubs play at Wrigley Field. Growing up in the Midwest, Oak Street Beach in downtown Chicago was the only beach I had known, and I never forgot how cool it was to be in a city one second and turn a corner and be at the beach. I decided I would try to find a hotel nearby and discovered a Four Seasons three blocks away. What were the odds it would be affordable? I checked anyway, and it turned out there was a special offer that put it within our reach. We decided to splurge, and I called the hotel.

"I understand you are traveling with children. Would you mind telling me their names and ages?"

I assumed the guy asked for my kids' ages to know whether they needed to banish us to a part of the hotel away from the adults. But their names? I couldn't figure that one out.

"Sure, but can you tell me why?"

"We like to address all of our guests by name. While we would refer to you and your wife as Mr. and Mrs., we will use your children's proper names."

Well, that sounded like a great explanation, so I didn't press on the age question, figuring I'd wait until I got there.

Upon arrival, a cheerful front-desk clerk welcomed Mr. and Mrs. Benjamin, then came around and kneeled down to address our kids, by name, at eye level.

I immediately realized what they were doing—creating an instant level of comfort. But that only works when done properly, with respect. Have you ever been to a restaurant where the server sits down at your booth as if you were pals? I have, and it's disturbing. The Four Seasons' first impression was intended to be a positive and lasting one for the whole family, and it was. But it didn't end there.

"Mr. Benjamin, we were actually able to provide you with an upgrade this weekend. Your suite has two bathrooms and is a corner lakeside. You should really enjoy the view."

Here was another takeaway: When you have an opportunity to provide additional service, do it! The suite we received was going to sit empty, so they gave us the upgrade at little additional cost to them. There are often times we should be able to do that in our restaurants, I thought, like when a deuce comes in on a relatively slow Monday night and there's an open four-top—let's give them the extra space!

When we entered the suite, the reason they'd asked the kids' ages was instantly apparent. I had already figured out that it couldn't have anything to do with segregating our family from adult guests, since we'd been given a prime location. Instead, sitting on the kids' beds were age-appropriate tour books of Chicago, and in the bathroom were a stool for my youngest to stand on while brushing her teeth plus two child-sized robes. I couldn't miss the fact that a little foresight goes a long way and made yet another note to bring back home: always give a little more. Typically when we stay in hotels I just lift my daughter over the sink to brush her teeth, and I would never have noticed the lack of a stool. But I sure noticed the little extra effort.

Of course, there are times when you may think you're going the extra mile, but in reality you've going a mile too far. In this case, I am referring the universal mistake of offering a kids' menu with the ubiquitous chicken fingers, French fries and PB&J. That delivers a very clear message that says, "We know you're here for the adults and the kids are just tagalongs, so we made a perfunctory attempt to keep them quiet while you enjoy yourselves."

When you think about it, the standard kids' menu described above is actually insulting to both the guests and the kitchen staff. Really, why would any restaurant have their well-trained cooks prepare a perfect pasta in a tremendously rich ragu of duck, and then also drop a few chicken fingers in the Fryolator?

Instead, why not create an atmosphere that invites the whole family to keep coming back as the kids get older? The Four Seasons Chicago did, in fact, have a kids' menu, but it was printed in the same font, on the same paper, and presented in the same leather holder as the adult menu. It featured great salads, a few pastas, fruits and some grilled items—all at reduced portions and prices.

What a great experience for the child who is used to having a box of crayons and a paper menu dropped in front of her!

If our experience in Chicago didn't grab my children's attention, what happened the following summer certainly did. We took a brief trip to Washington, DC, and since we were spared the expense of flying, decided to splurge again on a hotel. The Georgetown Four Seasons had a pretty high bar set for them, and boy, did they deliver. Upon arrival, they greeted our children by name. (I quickly made a note to self: share data between our restaurants so we can always address guests with familiarity when they visit our other locations.) Again there were gifts for the kids, a stool in the bathroom and a junior-sized but equally appointed menu in the dining room for the kids. One of our daughters was so happy she drew a picture for our server who, we later learned, immediately hung it up in his locker— as it turns out, the server knew one of our customers and texted him a picture of the work of art. Small world.

But the best lesson that day involved a correction to a major problem. The day before our arrival, the glass ceiling over the hotel's swimming pool had shattered in a hailstorm, rendering the pool useless for the length of our stay. While our kids would have enjoyed the pool, we found plenty of other things to do. It was no big deal, and the Four Seasons was not responsible for the hailstorm.

At checkout, the front desk manager asked, "Mr. Benjamin, are you heading back to Philadelphia this morning?"

"Yes, the kids have school tomorrow so we thought we would get home by lunch and relax for the rest of the day."

"That's a great idea. To make the relaxation part easier, I called the Four Seasons in Philadelphia. They would love to host you at their pool for the afternoon."

I couldn't believe it. We took them up on their offer and spent a fun afternoon by the pool. The Four Seasons gained a family of fans for life—if we hadn't been already—with one simple, unexpected gesture.

Speaking of the unexpected, I derived my most important rule of service from a character played by the late Patrick Swayze.

Just before staff training for the opening of our second restaurant, Osteria, having worked for several weeks with no break, I came home to rest. It had been nine years since I opened a restaurant, and various thoughts on how I would address this new staff were dancing around my head. I decided to take a break and turn on the TV, and when I did, one of my favorite cheesy movies came on. When I need to decompress, my favorite thing to do is to watch something that doesn't require me to think, but in this case I ended up thinking hard.

Road House is part chick flick, part tough guy action movie. I've watched it too many times to admit, but behind all the fistfights I suddenly saw a perfect little nugget of a lesson.

Swayze is a well-known bouncer—or "cooler"—hired to tame out-of-control bars around the country. He arrives at a joint that's been wracked with violence and drug dealing and is losing customers. On his first night there, he quietly observes, then calls a staff meeting to lay down the new rules. There's one that he repeats again and again, the simplest iteration of the Golden Rule: Be nice.

No matter what a customer says or does, be nice. Swayze goes through a bunch of scenarios in which rude, violent patrons challenge the bouncers, and for each of them, his bottom-line rule remains the same, with largely successful results.

Duly inspired, I broke out the expression many times in the next day's staff training session. And to this day, that simple phrase has been the primary message of every staff training session I've conducted, at every one of our restaurants.

I Hate Onions!

Genuine interest in each guest is the only way to go

I HATE ONIONS! What I mean is that I hate raw onions. And raw garlic, for that matter. And there's a very good reason why.

In the early nineties I was working in the business-dining division of what was then called ARA Services (now Aramark). My job was to operate the cafeteria at Citibank's world headquarters.

Occasionally, I was asked to assist in the executive dining rooms at 399 Park Avenue. Remember, this was the nineties—Sarbanes-Oxley hadn't passed yet and excess was the name of the game. The CEO had a private dining room with a table seating four, a dedicated server and a direct entrance from the kitchen.

One afternoon when I was working in the kitchen, I noticed that the CEO's table had been set. I was eager to see what was on the menu and watched as the chef gave careful instructions on how to create the elements of the meal—appetizer, salad, entrée, dessert. Incredibly, there were at least four people preparing lunch for two, in addition to other staff members who set the table. Abject excess aside, it was enlightening to see the care and thought that went into each aspect of this lunch. But it wasn't the ingredients that ended up on the plates that caught my eye; it's what didn't make it that mattered.

A new young cook had presented his dish, the salad course, and the chef just looked at it and froze. The room went silent as he addressed the young cook.

"Did you just make this salad?" he asked sharply.

"Yes, Chef."

"Can you tell me what's in it?"

"Yes, Chef. Field greens, heirloom tomatoes, diced red onions and beets, with balsamic vinegar on the side."

"Can you tell me what's wrong with that?"

The cook looked puzzled. "No, Chef."

"Can anyone in this kitchen tell me what's wrong with this salad?"

I was at a loss for words. It seemed like a perfectly normal salad. A little boring, perhaps—but wrong? I had no idea what the chef was getting at.

Another line cook spoke up. "Chef, there are raw onions in the salad."

"Very good! There are raw onions in the salad!" The chef turned to the cook. "Son, you were about to serve the CEO of one of the world's largest banks raw onions right before an afternoon of meetings with important clients. What would you think if you were sitting across the table from him and had to smell raw onion throughout a meeting? How does that reflect on us? You need to understand who you're serving. We aren't an assembly line. Thought goes into everything we do."

Thought goes into everything we do.

The line resonates to this day. It was a great learning experience to see such detailed, personal, next-level service. I also came to despise raw onions. I meet hundreds of guests each day and have no desire to greet them with onion breath. Every restaurant I go to, I let my server and everyone else know this restriction—but I only tell them once. It's up to them to read me and react. From cafés to four-star dining rooms, I expect the same standards I set for my own staff members. I like to know just how invested in my good time a staff is, or whether they're just phoning it in.

Often when Marc is working on a new dish, we'll deliver a sample to a regular guest's table as a little treat. It's our way of letting them know they're part of the family and that we value their opinion. Of course, our good intentions would be strewn along the road to hell if we were to thoughtlessly offer a plate of prosciutto to someone who always eats kosher, or send out shellfish stew to a regular whose shrimp allergy is common knowledge.

Even first-time guests we've never met will get this level of detail, inasmuch as we can give it. If someone's table isn't quite ready when they arrive, we may send out appetizers for the table on the house to thank them for their patience. And if no one in the group had ordered meat, we'd certainly not send out fazzoletti with duck ragu when the almond tortellini would be more appropriate.

Mistakes happen, of course. But it's a fine line between the occasional error and complacency. Any well-run restaurant will have ongoing training mechanisms in place that continually sharpen the service staff's skills in recognizing and responding to patrons' needs. This can't be accomplished by simply typing a guest's preferences into Open Table or the POS system. Being observant and taking a genuine interest is the only path to success.

When we dismiss or ignore a guest's cues, we're letting them know that they really only matter once. But success in this business is all about repeat customers. I've eaten in many restaurants where the food was really good, even great, but the service was lacking. I may not have made a conscious decision not to return, but the next time I dine out, that option likely won't occur to me.

As they say, there are too many fish in the sea—and for us, too many places cooking and serving them. That's why we have to stay on our toes.

Technophobia

Put down your phone and pick up the fork

WHEN I WAS A BOY, my friend Gordon and I would wash our neighbor's amazing car collection on weekends. Although he paid us for the work, we would have done it for free. One time while we were detailing his beautiful 1974 Jaguar XKE, I noticed a little switch under the dash labeled "Map" and flipped it on and off a couple times. Then I called Gordon over to play a little joke.

"Look, you flick this switch that says 'Map' and a small TV screen pops up with a map on it that tells you where to go."

"No way!" he replied.

I slowly moved my hand toward the dash, letting the drama build. "Are you ready?" I asked, and then flipped the switch. This being 1980, the only thing that happened was that a small overhead map light came on. We had a good laugh, and for years to come we would joke about the "TV map" that all expensive cars might someday have. Fast-forward to today, and virtually every new car has a built-in GPS on a screen with a map that tells you where to go!

I used to think that the restaurant business was technology-proof, that it was impossible to "virtually" experience what we do. Technological advancement affects every industry, including ours, and everyone is susceptible to the desire to pick up the latest gadget, then become addicted to it overnight. But in the restaurant business, it's crucial to consider each new tool carefully and make sure that we use it—or don't use it—for all the right reasons. That could mean shedding an old system to embrace new technology or rejecting a new toy because we realized it would actually detract from service. But more often than not, it means selectively using the new device's features to best suit your own needs.

A recent *New York Times* article detailed the efforts of one longtime restaurateur to figure out why all of his tables were taking longer to turn than they used to. His cooking and service methods had not changed, and staff consisted mostly of longtime servers. He considered all kinds of reasons, and then decided to watch two videos of a night of service—one from years ago and one from today—to search for evidence. The culprit quickly revealed itself. It was the cell phone.

Do I mean servers texting in the back when they should be serving up front? No, blame it on our guests. When they should be studying the menu, getting excited about the delicious food they're about to enjoy, they're checking sports scores. That's two minutes gone.

When the sweet onion crepe with fennel fonduta is placed on their table, instead of digging in, they take pictures of it for immediate upload to Instagram, Facebook and Pinterest—two more minutes down the drain. Then, when their entrée has been cleared, instead of perusing the desserts on the menu, they're getting in a quick game of Candy Crush. By the end of a cell-phone-riddled meal, anywhere from four to twelve minutes can be tacked on to the average table.

We did briefly discuss implementing some sort of cell phone restrictions in our dining rooms but quickly dismissed the notion. Since I became a father, I understand the need for quick access to the kids and the babysitter, and I know that trying to take people's cell phones away would be like trying to rip the gun out of Charlton Heston's "cold, dead hands."

The solution, as in so many other segments of this business, has been to adapt. We need to do whatever it takes to allow guests to have their phones and eat, too. If that means shaving off a minute here and there to bring table-turning times back to normal, that's what we do. Most of the time, when food service is paused because a guest has gone outside to take a call, we'll make a note to clear and reset the table quicker in between courses. There are many other ways to get things back on track without the guests even noticing.

Other new technologies save us considerable time every night, compared to how we used to do things. The POS system we use to input orders, track flow, gauge time lapses between courses, and much more is a far cry from its predecessor—paper and pencil. Open Table has also streamlined systems.

The iPad wine system used in all our restaurants is an incredible technological step forward, although I was slow to embrace it at first. The rep who sold it to us explained that every table can peruse our list on the iPad to be better prepared when we approach to take their order. This adds to the guest's experience by giving them more info about our cellar, while also cutting down on service time. But I stopped the salesman when he tried to sell me on the next step.

"The other great thing is that once the guest makes their choice, they just touch a button and their wine order goes directly to the POS. No fuss, no muss and your sommelier and server can focus on other duties."

No fucking way, I thought. But that's not what I said. Instead, I asked if that feature could be disabled—it could—and explained that while I love the idea of using the iPad as a tool to educate, I never want it to replace the valuable interaction between staff and guest.

We have worked hard to curate an extraordinary list, and our staff has a wealth of knowledge about it. Why would I want to deny guests the opportunity to take advantage of that knowledge? Often they arrive expecting to order a particular bottle but change their plans after a lively conversation with us. *That* is what I call an invaluable tool.

The iPad offered another feature that I vetoed immediately: Our POS system, it turns out, includes a paging feature connected to the iPad that would allow guests to summon their server at any time, for any reason, at the touch of a button. Can you imagine? Night after night of our guests' unreasonable expectations dashed, followed by bitter, lingering disappointment. Who needs that?

Our servers do a terrific job of fulfilling guests' needs swiftly, all night long. Each server works a minimum of five tables. What would make any guest think that paging a server would make them immediately stop what they were doing and come running on the spot? Let's be honest—that's exactly what most people would expect. Talk about a dangerous tool to put in the hands of every customer.

Still, we're hardly Luddites. At Pizzeria Vetri, guests can download our app and add their name to the wait list, find out how long it will be and let us know when they're running late. Clearly someone who worked in the restaurant business invented this particular app. The only thing it doesn't do is allow you to order.

While I am relatively sure that cars will ultimately drive themselves, something I may have mentioned to my friend Gordon back in 1980, I can hardly begin to anticipate the kinds of changes our business will see in the near future. Maybe guests will be able to order on their way to the restaurant, choosing options for seasoning and cooking methods. Maybe someone will invent self-cleaning tables and a sub-floor conveyor system that moves plates, glasses and silver to the kitchen and in the deluxe model, cleans it all on the way, like a car wash.

One thing I do know is that technology makes our world go faster and increases efficiency, while restaurants like ours exist to make you slow down, relax and savor a delicious, artful meal. At first, their union may seem counterintuitive, but when used in concert with each other, and allowing us to know our guests as well as ourselves, they can make beautiful music together at the table.

We Take the Blame

The customer is always right. Until they're wrong.

AND EVEN THEN, I take responsibility.

I've been blamed for the traffic. I've been blamed for the rain. I've been blamed for being on the wrong side of Broad Street. "How could you be all the way over here? This is ridiculous!" I've been blamed for sloping sidewalks, cracks in the sidewalk and flat tires. I've been blamed for late babysitters and rude parking lot attendants. I've been blamed for stomachaches (which turned out to be the flu). All of these woes are beyond my control, and I caused none of them. But for you, I will take the blame. I want you to be happy.

I can't fix the cracked sidewalk, but I can make you forget about your stubbed toe. I can't stop the rain, but you're in my shelter now, so sit for as long as you want with your dry martini. I can't thin out the traffic, but now that you're parked at our table, stick around for a while. We'll have an after-dinner drink. Let the traffic clear over a bowl of gelato. You'll be happy when you leave, if you let me try.

The customer may not always be right, but they're always the customer. If I can help them find a little bit of salvation at the end of a long day, even if it means swallowing a bit of pride in order to commiserate, then bring it on.

One miserably rainy night, a doctor arrived almost an hour late for his seven o'clock reservation. The rest of his party was close behind. It wasn't going to be a problem for us, until it was.

"Oh, I'm sorry," our host said when he announced himself. "I don't see your name here…"

He responded with ill humor, "I'm soaking wet. It's pouring rain. So I'm a little late. How did you think I was going to show up on time?"

Taken aback, the host tried to defuse the situation. "No, I was just saying I did not see your name at first, but I see it now in our seven o'clock slot. It's really not a problem, and I do apologize."

"You know, I had to wait forever in the rain in the parking lot for the attendant. How rude! Who do I talk to about that?"

"Sir, I'm sorry, but we do not own the parking lot and we don't have a business relationship with them. I'm happy to get you the company's phone number if you'd like."

"Fine," he said curtly, and then walked into the dining room, dipping wet. From the nearest empty table—which had just been set for the next party, which was not his—he grabbed some napkins and proceeded to dry himself off in the middle of the near-full dining room, where Marc and I had been standing. We wouldn't have believed it unless we'd seen it with our own eyes, but this gentleman proceeded to wipe himself down with our fancy linen. I ran over to him and said, "Sir, I have towels in the back. Please come with me and I'll bring some for you."

He continued to grab more linens, and said, "Oh, these will do just fine. But now I have to sit soaking wet. Do you have anything for me?"

I couldn't imagine what he was asking me for. A new outfit? A clothes dryer? I half-heartedly said, "Sir, I don't have anything to dry your clothes with, besides some towels."

He brushed off my offer, finished with the napkins, and said, "Oh, great. Fine. I guess I'll dry at some point, but your seats are going to get wet." I was fine with that.

The man accepted my invitation to take a seat at his table while waiting for his party, but before his butt hit the seat, he said, "Don't you have anything for me to drink?"

"Of course, we'll bring you something to drink. What would you like?"

"What do you have?"

"Everything that a normal bar has."

"Bring me a Johnny Walker Black on the rocks."

"Okay. What kind of water would you like?"

"What? Oh I don't care. Plain water."

We brought him his predinner cocktail, and soon enough the rest of his party appeared, thankfully a bit drier and more polite. They caught up with a drink, then placed their orders. We started to bring out the food. Throughout the meal, it was clear that there was nothing this gentleman liked, and worse, nothing we could do to make him happy. When the servers brought his third course, he looked up and sharply said "What is this?" as if they hadn't explained each of the previous courses as they were served.

All through the night, several of our staff dealt with this man, and handled him with grace and optimism, but were met at each turn with growls, grimaces and general disdain.

By dessert—which makes most people really happy—he had actually warmed up a little. His clothes were dry, the parking lot incident was a distant memory and whatever business he was doing with the people at his table seemed to have been successful. After he paid the check, he stood up, looked at us, smiled thinly and said, "Everything was wonderful, thanks."

We were happy to have the thanks. We were happy everything was wonderful. How about an apology? That was not going to happen. Sometimes we just have to suck it up in the service industry; that's what service professionals do.

I didn't grow up in the restaurant business; I grew up in the religion business. As the son of a rabbi, I was taught to take a different perspective on life's challenges. When my friends' parents were meting out corporal punishment at home, my transgressions were met with the teachings of Aristotle, Plato and Descartes— words of wisdom to provide direction around life's little roadblocks.

One story has remained an inspiration over the years, and I've retold it during our preservice meetings to remind staff of one of their most important responsibilities.

It's the story of the trouble tree. A once-grand old temple was starting to show wear and tear around the façade, so a few handymen were hired to paint walls and repair broken windows. After a particularly grueling day, the rabbi noticed the last worker packing up to leave. He also noticed that the only car in the lot was his own, and assumed the man was walking home. He approached this weary man and offered him a ride.

"But Rabbi," the man replied. "You don't know where I live. What if it's out of your way?"

"Well, the car does all the work; all I have to do is steer! I'm getting ready to leave for the day, too. We'll enjoy the ride together."

The man accepted the rabbi's offer and off they went. They talked about the work being done on the temple, the challenges the laborer had faced that day and how much longer the job might take. They pulled up to the man's house, and as the rabbi said goodbye, the man said, "You know, there's always extra food at our dinner table. Why don't you join us? I'd love for you to meet my family, and I would like to repay you for taking me home and saving me the long walk."

The rabbi accepted. At the doorway, the man stopped and bent over a sickly little tree full of branches but devoid of leaves. He rubbed his hands on several of the branches, stood up and continued to the door, his smile growing. After a quick glance back at his guest, he threw open the door and yelled, "Daddy's home!" Three kids ran up and jumped into his arms. His wife walked over, kissed him on the cheek and and asked, "So how was your day?"

"Just great. We got a lot of work done, and we are all set for tomorrow's project. By the way, I've invited a dinner guest—the rabbi of the temple I'm working on. I hope it's okay."

"Of course it's okay. You know I always make too much food! Come on in, Rabbi."

The rabbi shook her hand and said hello to the kids. In the back of his mind he was contemplating, *How could this man, exhausted from a hard day's work, be so cheerful once he entered the door? What a wonderful way to live!*

They shared a great meal, had some laughs and the time came for the rabbi to leave. The man walked him to the door, opened it and escorted him out. As the rabbi reached the sickly tree that the man had deliberately rubbed earlier, curiosity got the better of him.

"I couldn't help but notice that you rubbed this tree on the way in."

"Oh that? That's my trouble tree."

"Your trouble tree?"

"You see, Rabbi, I often have frustrating days where things happen that weigh on my mind. I guess I'm no different from most people in that regard. But since I get to spend so little time with my family, I need to make sure I am fully *with* them when I am with them, if you know what I mean."

The rabbi nodded.

"So on my way home after work, I rub all of my troubles off of me and onto the tree branches. When I leave for work in the morning, I stop back and pick them up. The funny thing is, there are never as many troubles on the tree in the morning!"

I like to think of us in the hospitality business as a trouble tree. We never know what kind of mood customers will be in when they arrive at our restaurant. On a basic level, we have to assume that they are out for enjoyment after a long day facing their own set of roadblocks. Whatever their particular circumstances, it is one of our many jobs to do all we can to let their troubles rub off. A happy guest is generally easy to please, but an unhappy guest, well, that's the challenge. To see a guest who came in downtrodden leave with a smile—there's just nothing like it.

We are in the happiness business. No matter what challenges lie in wait outside our restaurant doors, we are there to provide relief while you are behind them.

And on your way out, feel free to leave some of your troubles at the coat check.

Help Us Help You

Once we start touching them, they're ours

I LOVE STANDING on the front porch at Vetri right before opening, greeting guests as they arrive and wishing them a good dinner as they step inside our home.

The earlier we make our first impression, the better. Everything we say and do, from hello to good-bye, will contribute to whether a guest has a memorable experience or a night they'd rather forget. Similarly, everything they say to us about their experience in real time will make their evening better. The lesson is that once we start touching them, they're ours.

One recent evening I was on the porch with Marc, greeting guests. Everyone seemed pleased, even genuinely excited to be there. You'd think I'd be thrilled, right?

"You know," I said to Marc, "nothing makes me happier than to see these nice people looking forward to a great meal. But at the same time, nothing makes me more nervous."

Marc laughed. "Why?" he asked.

"Well, when they arrive in a *bad* mood—whether they had a long day or just had to fight through a traffic jam to get here—there are so many opportunities for us to turn that around. The atmosphere inside those doors will lift their spirits. They'll receive a warm greeting and attentive service. Expert wine service will stimulate their mind. And of course, your food is going to blow them away. It's almost like shooting fish in a barrel.

"But when somebody arrives in the best of moods, with the expectation that we will take them even higher, well," I looked at the chef, paused for a moment, and said, "You better go in that kitchen right now and wow those people!"

"You'd better get to work, too," he replied with a smile as he turned to go inside.

It's usually pretty obvious when a guest is enjoying their evening. The challenge is figuring out when they're not. Communication may be a two-way street, but the reality is that many people—for many reasons—keep their discomfort to themselves because they don't want to speak up. They'll slog through a dish they don't really like, or leave half of it on the plate. They'll deal with a wobbly table and the minor annoyance that brings. They'll eat food that's too salty for their taste. Who knows what else they will suffer in silence.

If I could impart one piece of advice to guests, it is this: On the rare occasion that you don't like something, anything, about your experience, please speak up and tell us. Even if there's something you can't quite articulate, don't worry—we really don't need an explanation. To us, the only thing worse than causing you any measure of unhappiness is having you *choose* to leave unhappy without telling us.

A dish is too peppery for your liking? You ordered strozapretti thinking it was as thin as angel hair? You thought you had ordered one dish, actually ordered another, but really wanted the one you thought you had ordered? You asked for octopus salad but we sent out octopus pizza? Tell us; you will now enjoy both.

We can and do read many of your behavioral cues throughout

the night, and we react accordingly. But we can't read minds. There will always be a certain amount of information that's incumbent upon the guest to relay.

I can't tell you how many times I've heard from diners in the days after they ate with us that not everything was perfect. Perfection is most definitely our goal. We usually achieve it in most people's minds. But for others, it's only possible if we know where we may be falling short.

Though I understand the reluctance to complain, I'd rather recook every dish we serve than hear, days later, the line that keeps me up at night. "Oh, I just didn't want to complain." And: "Everything else was excellent. I just didn't like that one dish, so no big deal." And: "The rest of my group loved it and they told me to send mine back, but I just said, 'It's fine; forget it.'"

You don't need to cause a scene in order to make your needs known to someone on staff. If you feel your steak is undercooked, simply telling us is much more dignified for all involved than angrily calling over the server and grumbling, "What is this, sushi?"

A subtle gesture or meeting of eyes is all it takes to get our attention. More often than not, your server will be checking in on you within moments after you've discovered that you need something, so waiting a few seconds is also an option. Like any other human interaction, the more respect you give, the more you will receive.

Don't worry about how the kitchen will feel when you send back a dish. Hollywood has done a major disservice to restaurant service, as we can all picture the standard scene where a chef is told that a customer was not happy with a dish, picks up a butcher knife and heads toward the dining room to set the record straight, only to be held back by the nervous line cooks. I hesitate to even address the disgraceful myth that a dish sent back will be returned with more ingredients than normal, if you know what I mean. Trust me: tampering with food never, ever happens. Every person on staff, including those handling food in the back of the house, operates with the sole purpose of elevating your enjoyment and impressing the hell out of you while doing so.

The reason we want to make everything better for you is not to uphold our reputation in the future, but to exceed your expectations of us in the present. So talk to us. We won't bite.

How We Met the Capolinos

You've heard of repeat guests? I'm talking hundreds of times.

I'VE ALWAYS SAID that we are in the relationship-building business. Everything we do and say regarding guests is intended to not only make the night at hand special, but also to lay a foundation for many more special nights in the future.

For some guests, all it takes to gain their repeat business is courteous service and enjoyable food; they may have no expectation or desire for longer conversations or a personal relationship, and that's just fine. Yet others may be open to something more.

Vetri had been operating for just a couple of months when Peter and Fran Capolino came in. They lived nearby and were interested to see what was going on inside the newest restaurant in their neighborhood. After they had been seated, I stopped by their table and they asked about a wine. At the time, I had curated a relatively small list of about eighty bottles, mostly Italian selections, but I was confident in what we had to offer and my familiarity with each bottle.

Well, one question led to two, and before long we were engaged in lively conversation. Fran had a clear understanding of the Italian wine world; she wasn't an expert, but didn't claim to be, either, so it was very nice to educate her but also to hear about what she liked and why. The three of us ended up talking through most of the wine list together.

At one point, Fran stopped and said, "You know what, why don't you choose our wine tonight. What do you suggest?"

"I can't really suggest a wine for you." I smiled, and then finished my thought, "Well, not before asking a few questions."

They talked about the wines they typically like and described a few great bottles they had recently enjoyed. I asked what they felt like eating that night, and they had a pretty good idea. They also wanted to try something different yet still in the wheelhouse of the flavor profile and quality they preferred, a multicourse wine that would hold up to a variety of dishes.

I held out the wine list and pointed to a bottle of Argiolas.

Peter scanned the page, looked at me quizzically and said, "We can afford a better bottle than that."

It's true that the bottle I had suggested was on the lower end of the price scale. But with everything we had just discussed, it seemed the best choice. Obviously, price was not one of the factors in my suggestion; it rarely is.

"It has nothing to do with the price. You've asked me to choose something appropriate, and although we've just met, I have really enjoyed our conversation and think that you will be pleasantly surprised. I wasn't trying to suggest what you can afford, one way or the other! This is the right bottle for tonight."

They smiled and came to quick agreement. "Well, if that's the case, go get that bottle!" he said.

That evening we talked about the wine, among other things. I still remember the conversation distinctly. The bottle was from Sardinia, an island where winemakers primarily use a grape called Cannonau. That grape is very similar to Grenache, which is more familiar to Americans. In discussing the geographic provenance of several grapes, our conversation veered toward the different places we had visited. At the end of the evening, we thanked each other for the conversation, and they remarked that the wine was good on its own, but even better with the education that came with it.

After that we started seeing the Capolinos regularly, probably twice a week. We all shared a great passion for food and wine, which is really a love of people. Many nights they spent as much time talking to me and our staff as they did to each other. It turned out that Peter and I were both sports nostalgia fans. In fact, he owned a sporting goods company that had outfitted the Philadelphia Eagles. He understood my undying love for the Chicago Cubs, and humorously commiserated when I admitted that they'd probably never win a championship.

Fast forward fifteen years, and Peter and Fran still visit one of our restaurants almost every night of the week. They always ask me to select their beverage, whether it's a bottle of wine at Vetri, a beer at Alla Spina or a cocktail at Amis. By now, our friendship has outgrown the walls of our restaurants. We have shared many meals in other places. Our families have traveled together and attended basketball games and baseball games. All of this grew out of their original request for me to make a wine selection, their appreciation of my thoughtful suggestion and the fact that both sides were open to allowing a relationship to slowly grow.

Of course, it didn't really matter whether we bonded in those first moments. What mattered was that we clicked on the level of service, and we built on that professional relationship until it became a friendship. Naturally, you can't do that with every guest; most, after all, are interested in talking to each other. But sometimes, when you do provide excellent service, you may just gain a friend for life.

I've always said that we can easily get someone to eat at one of our restaurants once. The question is whether they come back. In the case of the Capolinos, they've come back thousands of times over the years and have really become members of our family. To this day, Argiolas reminds me warmly of them. To a small degree, it's great that I made a perfect wine choice that night. But more importantly, I made some great friends. And in the relationship-building business, that's a win-win.

What's Old Is New Again

Trends come and go, but farm to table should not be a passing fad

SO HOW DO WE AVOID the dreaded one-night stand and keep people coming back again and again? Excellent service is one factor. Stellar food is another. But the key to ongoing long-term patronage is the slightly less obvious fact that we have to constantly change and grow to keep things fresh, new and exciting for our guests. The bonus is that doing so also keeps things fresh and exciting for ourselves.

You might think that after two decades in this industry, most of them self-employed, I'd be able to provide a little insight into what the future will hold for the restaurant world. "What new trends do you expect to see this year?" people ask me. And I always answer, "I have absolutely no idea!"

I know that isn't the best answer, but it's the truth. Sure, we can and do consider various media reports, market research and activity in the rest of our industry when we're creating a new menu or contemplating changes in service or restaurant design. However, as I like to say, "Man plans, and God laughs."

Although the high-protein, low-carb Atkins Diet was inspired by a medical paper from 1958 and first published by Dr. Robert Atkins in 1972, it didn't grab much media attention until 2002 when a revised edition of Atkins's book caused the diet to soar past the level of mere trend to become a national craze. Who saw that coming? I've always been curious to know how many people opened bakeries in 2002 only to have the low-carb fad sweep the nation and throw them out of business.

Today's version of such a trend is the gluten-free diet. While I am fully aware that a very real affliction called celiac disease affects a small portion of the population, the number of people I have met who voluntarily gave up gluten because they simply believe it is a healthier way to live boggles my mind. Talk about a trend that I didn't see coming! As someone who makes his living selling pasta and pizza, the gluten-free diet can be the kiss of death. So imagine my dismay when we opened Pizzeria Vetri just when this trend started to hit its stride.

Would we have discarded plans for our fast-casual pizza restaurant if we'd noticed the trend sooner? Probably not. Despite the fact that over a million and a half Americans have gone gluten-free without so much as a diagnosis, most everyone still loves pizza.

When I talk to young people entering the hospitality business, or to reporters interviewing me on the state of its economy, I stress the importance of always knowing where we've been and frequently glancing ahead at where we're going. We run trend reports just like any other business. How did we perform this year compared to last year, and this quarter over last quarter? What was the effect of last year's snowy winter versus the previous year's virtually snow-free season? We will continue to crunch all such numbers. However, when the question is asked, I know that the asker is looking for the next big thing in food

In all of our restaurants, we are fanatical about keeping the menus fresh and exciting. That's what keeps our regular guests coming back again and again over the years. But we don't necessarily do trends. Instead, we follow our hearts. So when our culinary team sits down to throw out blue-sky ideas for the newest thing, their sources can come from literally anywhere. That's why, so many times, they surprise me.

I walked into Vetri a few months back and found Marc and chef Adam Leonti designing the next season's menu. The surprise wasn't the fact that they were meeting on such matters; it happens almost weekly. The a-ha moment was when I noticed the two cookbooks that Adam was using as reference. One of them was from the fifth century, and the other one was much more recent, having been published in 1582!

Of course, I figured they knew what they were doing, but still couldn't pass up the opportunity to comment on the irony. "Are you guys working on the menu for *next year* or *last century?*"

Adam was clearly energized. "These are the roots of Italian cooking! This book is the first-known instance of Italians writing down their processes. There are recipes in here for items that we cook now. How cool is that!"

You would've thought that he'd discovered a brand-new method, but instead he'd found notes on the oldest methods known to mankind. From this revelation, he and the rest of the culinary group developed a new seasonal menu, including new (to us) ingredients and methods of cooking and preparation. In fact, we now mill our own flour using a technique that existed long before automation. And what a difference it's made.

I've seen many fads come and go, and it's always interesting to trace the trends back to things that we've all done before. As I write this, there are new burger restaurants popping up all over the place. Of course, burgers have been a mainstay in our culture since Ray Kroc said, "Hey, we can scale this idea" and created McDonald's. And like Mickey D's secret sauce, today's burger joints all have to come up with some new angle or twist in order to compete. Interestingly, many have sprouted out of a fine-dining sensibility, and so they're using ingredients that have likely never been used before in burgers—or so we may think.

Similarly, there's a trend of new pizza restaurants (despite the concurrent gluten-free trend) serving pies the likes of which haven't been seen commercially in America, and creating a mid-casual alternative to the popular chains that have owned the market since the 1970s. We like to think that we've gotten out in front of the curve by opening Pizzeria Vetri a couple years ago. But when we started doing research, we found that this is nothing new. Our culinary team traveled extensively through Italy to meet with some storied pizzaiolos there, and we sent chef Brad Spence to a pizza-making class. Ultimately, none of this positioned us to do anything revolutionary. In fact, it would be silly to suggest that revisiting a centuries-old process is breaking new ground; we're just following in the footsteps of those who came before.

One recent trend drives me crazier than all the rest: farm to table, used by everyone and their grandmother starting in the late '90s. It's been so overused that I once said to Marc, "If any marketing collateral ever leaves our company with the term 'farm to table' on it, I quit!"

Farm to table is the way all restaurants, at one time, did operate, and how all restaurants today should operate. But with the advent of industrial changes like preservatives, canning, long-range transportation and large-scale commercial food production, plus the societal embrace of fast food, quick-serve, microwave meals and eating at our desks, that reality changed, and the opposite became the trend. For the longest time, the phrase "farm to table" didn't exist, but the concept did—it was simply called food. At this point in the evolution of the industry, it would be foolish not to operate as a farm to table operation. Just don't build a marketing campaign around the slogan, "We have food!"

I recently entered a local outlet of one of the hot new burger chains and had to chuckle at the sign that read, "All of our vegetables are sourced from local farms, and all of our French fries are hand-cut from locally grown potatoes daily."

What's old is new again, indeed.

PART FOUR

THE STAFF

*The truth is, we may appear like a raft
of ducks gliding across the surface
while in fact we are paddling like hell.*

Welcome to the Family

An employer is more than just the guy who signs the paycheck

IN LATE 2013, WE OPENED our first restaurant outside Philadelphia. The fact that it's in a suburban mall in Moorestown, New Jersey, raised some eyebrows on the local food scene. Only fifteen miles from Philly, we were moving into uncharted territory—suburbia—and becoming de facto retail folks.

Not only was a sizable portion of the local customer base unfamiliar with us, but so was the hiring pool. Up to that point, all of our restaurants were located within a mile of each other in Center City and drew from the same group of workers for staffing. Every potential employee had heard of us, if not dined with us at some point. They knew what Vetri stood for. For some reason, we hadn't anticipated the fact that hiring staff in Moorestown would have to begin with an explanation of who we were, and it gave us pause. The fact is, we hang our hat on our name and it usually requires no explanation.

Some years ago, when we needed to come up with a corporate identity, we started throwing out ideas. When the name "Vetri Family" was floated, Marc gave instant approval with his trademark expression, "Boom!" He got it out a moment before I could; we both knew that nailed it. While Vetri Family works as our corporate name, it represents much more. It's a way of life, and a way of running a business. We are more than just a group of people who work together. From our beginnings with a staff of just twelve to our current staff of well over four hundred, we continue to thrive on that mentality. We care about each other inside and outside the restaurant, and while we argue like any other family, we would also lie down on a railroad track for each other. So when someone on our staff gets married, has a baby, buys a house or achieves one of life's dreams, we all share in the joy.

But how do you communicate such a deep-rooted sensibility to a brand new staff that had barely heard of us and had no idea about how we operate? I'm sure that some of them had preconceived notions, and I can imagine the thought process: "I've seen Marc Vetri on TV. He's one of those star chefs and probably has a huge ego. I bet they think they're going to come in here and change the world."

We knew we couldn't just show up and say, "We're a family; come join us." So we approached it as an opportunity to hit the reset button and examine how we interact with every member of our group. In training the Moorestown staff, we retrained ourselves in defining and describing who we are. We share a common goal to serve guests with the utmost hospitality, to prepare and deliver the highest-quality food and to create an experience that guests will want to enjoy again and again.

Last but certainly not least, we want to create an employee experience that far transcends the typical restaurant world scenario.

Once in the early days of Vetri, I walked into the kitchen to find Marc reading an old book by the famous French chef Fernand Point. He showed me a line in the book that said in order to be a successful chef, one must treat the dishwasher with the same respect as anyone else on staff. Marc took that to heart, and the concept took hold to shape what we've become. After all these years, and despite so much success, that basic humility remains.

In our first week at Osteria Moorestown, we had some good news and some bad news. The good news was that we were incredibly busy; the bad news was that we didn't staff the kitchen properly to handle the volume. The dishwashing staff in particular struggled to keep up. While I stood in the kitchen talking with a manager and trying to come up with a plan, I turned to see a guy take his place next to the other dishwashers and start getting his hands wet. It was Marc Vetri.

It was not a showboating move, nor a photo op. He wasn't trying to teach anybody a lesson. He got in there because it had to be done. And he didn't just simply wash the dishes. In minutes he was talking to the guys, offering ideas and creating an assembly line. "Hey, what if we put the dirty dishes here to create more space over there for the pots? Why don't you do the pots, you do the dishes and during the busy time I'll come back and help polish glasses." He stayed for as long as it took to get things back on track.

That action spoke more to the meaning of Vetri Family than any platitudes we may have repeated to the staff at a team meeting. It showed that Marc was there not just to help them, but also to help them help themselves. It meant that he was invested in *their* success. Once everyone heard that the owner of the restaurant showed up and washed dishes, they realized that our message was sincere. Of course, I now joke that the highest-paid department during an opening is the dish staff!

I had a similar experience when we opened the original Osteria in Philadelphia. You've probably guessed by now that I've never really gotten away from the idea of being a server—I loved doing it when I was at that country club on Long Island years ago, and I loved doing it early on in our own restaurants. Service is still my favorite thing to do, to be honest. There's nothing more invigorating than walking up to a table and talking to a guest, helping them through the menu, assisting with their wine choice and providing everything they need to relax and enjoy a great evening.

By the time we opened the first Osteria, our staff had grown to more than fifty but I still felt like we were a tight-knit group of twelve. The dynamic between managers and servers had changed, but apparently no one told me! One night, I saw a table of four get seated just as their server began taking orders at a larger table across the room. Since it is our practice to show up at each table within a minute of seating to greet the guests, provide menus and answer any questions, I quickly decided to help out. I approached, handed out menus, chatted them up a bit, and before I knew it, I was taking their orders and entering them into the computer system for the kitchen to see. Within minutes, the appetizers were up and we started delivering the food. All of a sudden I look over and see the server talking to our general manager, obviously distraught. When they separated, I walked over to the manager and asked, "What's wrong?"

"You know, Jeff, I don't think you should have taken that order at Table Four."

"What are you talking about?" I replied, genuinely puzzled. "That's what we do! We take orders, we send them to the kitchen, the orders come out and we serve the table. I mean, how else do you expect the kitchen to know what to make?"

"It's not that *we* shouldn't have taken the order," he said, "it's that *you* shouldn't have taken the order. The server now thinks that you think he did something wrong."

"Well, that's strange. Where does it say that when you offer to help one of your coworkers, it really means that they did something wrong?"

I just couldn't fathom that. But in any case, that wasn't the impression I wanted to make, so I walked over to talk to the server.

"You know, I was just trying to help you out, that's all," I said. "I saw that you were busy with other guests when Table Four got seated, so I stepped in to cover for you and get them started. You didn't do anything wrong."

He replied, "At all of my other jobs, if a manager came over and took an order, that meant we were doing something wrong."

"Well, in the Vetri Family, if a manager—or even an owner, for that matter—comes over and takes an order, it doesn't mean that. In fact, if any of your coworkers—manager, owner or otherwise—doesn't help you out, *they* are the ones doing something wrong. We are a team."

Over the years we have promoted that theory, and admittedly, we have made some mistakes. I don't think I have treated every employee the way I would want to be treated, and I think that's human. But I believe that our employees think of me as a coworker despite the fact that I own the company, and that they know I would do anything for them. It isn't enough to ensure you pay a living wage, which I hope we do. It is the dignity with which you approach your team that matters.

Whenever our restaurants face slow times, like in the middle of the summer or particularly harsh winters, hours can be hard to come by for the staff. In those times I'll approach a team member and say, "Hey, thanks for weathering the storm. You know, next week is looking up." They get the gist of my message and usually say something like, "I'm not bailing, I love it here."

Many times people apply for a job with us while earning more elsewhere. When I tell them up front, "I'm sorry, but at the level we are looking to hire, we just can't meet your previous salary," the response is typically, "I really want to work for the Vetri Family. I know I'll get to where I was. Until then I need to love my job."

An employer is more than just the guy who signs the paycheck. Currently there is national debate over minimum wage and tipping practices. I have my opinions, but at the end of the day, business owners, at least the ones I come in contact with, do their best to ensure that employees are fairly compensated. But the fact that there is disagreement means they've failed in other ways to make their staff happy.

I have left several jobs myself where I initially thought my reason for leaving was salary, but when I reflected further, I left because I didn't like the job and the company. A raise would have simply paid me more to do an unsatisfying job, and it was only a matter of time before I left. When I felt a company wasn't invested in me, I knew it was time to go. Now I know—and Marc knows, too—that you need to invest in employees beyond just handing them a check. Good business owners know their staff and are ready to help them in any way possible.

About a year ago, I heard several employees talking about saving to buy houses. I called a mortgage broker friend and asked him to host a seminar for the staff about how to buy a house. It was well attended, and within the year four attendees had bought their own homes. I was almost as excited as they were.

We have welcomed many babies to the Vetri family over the years, and nothing makes me happier than to know that, from a medical standpoint, the new parents were able to concentrate on the important part because of our employee insurance plan. In our second year, I'd been thinking about employee health insurance—which is not common in the restaurant industry—and brought up the idea with Marc. He said, "Absolutely, if you can find affordable health care for our staff, let's do it." We provide insurance for all employees on a fifty-fifty basis to start, and once they reach management level, we cover 100 percent.

Recently, with a group of restaurant colleagues, I discussed the struggle of adjusting budgets to comply with the Affordable Care Act when it goes into effect in the coming year. It was never even debatable to us; it was just the right thing to do. And for years it's been one of the factors that sets us apart from other restaurants.

Another is our matching 401(k) program. When we realized that our staff was staying longer than the industry average and that some of them may ultimately retire with us, the obvious next step was to offer a retirement plan. It's gratifying to encourage employees to start saving for the future. To date, more than one-third of our staff is involved in the plan. We hope to continue to offer this matching program forever, even if it means less money today for us.

There are many other things an employer can do to create meaningful impact for employees without taking a financial hit to the company. We recently implemented the Vetri Family Newsletter to highlight births, marriages, home purchases and other events worth celebrating. It also reports promotions within the company, which really instills a sense of opportunity within the team. We also throw a party every year for the staff. It's always a great time.

Obviously all of these gestures cost us money, time and energy. But such investments also bring amazing returns. Whatever you do as an employer, always remember that your key to success lies in the success of the team—both at work and away from the job. Never take that for granted.

Cast of Characters

The chef is the quarterback. But let's not forget the dish staff, shall we?

ON A TYPICAL evening, you—the diner—usually come in contact with just a few members of our staff: host, servers, food runners, maître d', sommelier and, on occasion, the manager or captain. Once in a while you may get a visit from the chef. But there are back-of-house staff involved in the orchestration of your evening whom you may never see, though their interaction with the front is crucial. Together, we do everything we can to make your whole night seem effortless. The truth is, we are like a raft of ducks appearing to glide serenely across the surface, while in fact we are paddling like hell to keep moving forward!

Foremost, of course, is the chef. He or she is the face of the restaurant, the menu creator, the food-cost manager and the person on whose shoulders the whole enterprise rests. To use a football analogy, the chef is the quarterback. In our organization, chef Marc Vetri is also the founder and CEO, so he has a vested interest in the outcome of each guest's visit—not to mention the success of every team member.

Early on I realized that Marc's interest reached beyond the kitchen doors. He enters the dining room nightly not just to make the perfunctory appearance, but to really gauge the mood of the room. Is the music too loud or not loud enough? Is that couple in the corner enjoying themselves? Is the lighting perfect, or does it need adjustment? How is the birthday celebration going at Table Six? All these questions are no less important to Marc than the quality of the food leaving the kitchen. Any restaurant that achieves such ongoing success likely has a quarterback chef like Marc.

The second most important player on a football team is the line-man, who protects the quarterback's blind side. In the restaurant business, that person is called the expediter. The "expo" station is the hub to which all spokes of the wheel connect.

You know that chefs, sous chefs and line cooks prepare the food, and service staff delivers orders to the kitchen and food to the guests. But how does it all happen in sync? How does the kitchen know which dishes to cook and when? How do they know which plates to send up next? How do the servers know which plates sitting in the window are theirs to deliver? And what do the servers do when a food issue comes up at one of their tables that threatens to throw everything out of whack? The answer to all of the above is simple: Ask the expo.

It is the expediter's job to stand in the kitchen at an area called the pass and process every order with precision and efficiency, ensuring that all dishes finish cooking simultaneously so every guest gets their food as hot and on-time as the rest of their party. Virtually all guests follow the unwritten social rule that no one eats until everyone has been served. We all know what it's like to have three people sitting with their plates in front of them while the fourth is waiting for her entrée. It is the expo's job to make sure that never happens.

Different restaurants have their own ways of running the pass. Some designate cooks responsible for specific items—one person cooking all pasta, another doing all grill items or cold items and so on. When a table needs something from each, the expo coordinates the cooks so they get their item—protein, veg, etc.--up at the same time. In some classic kitchens, the expo actually finishes all plates with the sides, but that system is becoming a rarity. Either way, the expo is the person tasked with controlling the flow of orders in and dishes out. Sounds easy, right?

Imagine you are the expo and a server suddenly informs you that one of the four top at Table Two just changed his mind, so the other three plates, just being completed, now have to wait. At the same time one of your cooks says he ran out of the special you just ordered for Table Three. Then your food runner returns with all four dishes you just sent out to Table Four because one guest is in the bathroom and we don't partially serve a table. You can't ask the chef for help because you are protecting his blind side; if you went to him with every such situation, it would grind the pass to a halt. You don't want to waste any food, but you also don't want anyone's food to be imperfect. So what do you do?

First, you get the manager to tell the server with the canceled special to take an order for something else and in the meantime you grab the amazing pasta dish that just got returned from Four and won't hold up during the guest's bathroom break, put Four's other three dishes under heat and send the pasta as a gift to the guest waiting for the special replacement at Three along with that table's three other dishes (not forgetting to have the pasta cook fire up another one for Four).

Then you order the change for Two, tell the cooks to place Two's three other plates under heat as soon as they finish and tell the manager to tell the server to tell the guests at Two how much longer that new order will take (reassuring them that it is absolutely no problem). Talk about a juggling act. If you pull it off, there's no time to celebrate—another situation is probably right around the corner.

When things in the front of the house veer toward chaos, the person who rights the ship is called the captain—literally. The captain is there for the servers, constantly on the lookout for any issues that threaten to disrupt the flow. If a server gets caught up at a table of eight where none of the guests can decide what they want, she may throw a look toward the captain to check on another table that's on the verge of waiting too long. Since he has a firm grip on the whereabouts of each table's flow, he'll know exactly what her look means and will step in and bridge the gap. He will have already anticipated it. And when that problem is solved, he'll already know what the next one is going to be.

On a broader scale, the maître d' oversees the entire room from a strategic sense as well as an interactive one. He's never far from the table chart, which he revises throughout the evening to maximize the number of people we can serve while minimizing wait times, if any, for all guests. He also walks the room and stops by tables to ask how people are doing, Like the rest of us, he takes his cues from the guests' needs, whether they're implied or expressed, and does so seamlessly by offering just the right amount of conversation with just the right tone.

Another visitor some guests will receive is the sommelier. The house beverage expert does not approach every table, but she will notice guests who are spending time perusing the wine, spirits or beer list and come over to engage them. More often than not, however, guests will ask their server for a conversation with the sommelier. She'll quickly note their level of expertise and direct conversation based on that. She allows those who clearly know wine to express that knowledge while adding to the conversation based on her own expertise. Those who admit to knowing very little about wine she will guide toward the perfect bottle based on a few simple questions.

Either way, the sommelier's conversation is always a two-way street and never a one-way speech. She wants to know what you know and what you love, and ultimately, if you do ask her to make a suggestion, she wants to do it based on the context that you provided. Of course, once in a while she will come face to face with someone who thinks they know what they're talking about, but really don't. For instance, the guy who says he's having bucatini with jalapeño and almond pesto and wants to pair it with a bottle of Amarone. With great tact, she will steer him away from that particular choice by pointing out the volatile mix of spicy food with high alcohol content, and suggest a better pairing. Whatever you are drinking, I encourage every guest to engage their sommelier, even when they already know what they want. Like most things in life, the more you know about something, the more likely you will enjoy it.

The host is the first person you see on arrival, so his or her job is to put you at ease, let you know when you'll be seated (if not immediately) and instill a sense of confidence that all is well. But that's not all the host does. You will often see her at the computer, rearranging table configurations to accommodate scheduled guests as well as the last-minute walk-ins, no-shows and late arrivals. It's like working on a jigsaw puzzle whose pieces are always changing; never underestimate one piece of the puzzle.

As you glance around the room you may glimpse the barista tracing a funny design in the cappuccino foam; a busser swiftly resetting a table for guests who have been patiently waiting at the bar; runners exiting the pass with equal measures of speed and dexterity on their way to tables. To the naked eye, all appears smooth and right with the world.

Meanwhile, back in the kitchen, you don't see some of the most important members of the team: the dish staff. The average guest presumes there is an endless supply of clean dishes and utensils available at all times. (It is probably this presumption that explains why relatively law-abiding citizens have a penchant for taking silverware from restaurants.) Imagine, however, if a server arrived at your table and announced, "The dish staff is a little overwhelmed tonight, so it's going to be a while for new silverware," or "You'll need to use the same glass for wine and water tonight because our dish staff didn't come to work today. I'm sure you won't mind." Actually, I'm sure you wouldn't tolerate it.

I've heard people use the understaffed excuse to explain lengthy delays in other stores and industries. It wouldn't fly here. Most of us take it for granted, and wrongfully so. It doesn't *just happen,* so these guys do deserve some credit if not acknowledgement. The fact is, you can't just walk into a dish room and start washing. There is a system, like everything else, and to do the job well one needs to be smart and attuned to everything going on around them. "Are we low on glassware for the bar?" "Is the silverware all set?" "Does the kitchen need new sauté pans for the second turn, and if so, should we stop dish cleaning and scrub pans instead right now?" Addressing such questions may be sausage-making at its finest, because no guest ever wants know anything about the dish room, although they sure expect it to be running efficiently. Sometimes, it gets so crazy that the boss has to step in and get his hands wet, too.

The one person I haven't mentioned yet is the one with whom guests have the most interaction throughout the night—and that's the server. From a guest's perspective, it's probably the most intriguing position in the restaurant. And for the purposes of this book, it's a chapter all its own.

The Hospitality Gene

Great waiters are born, not made

EVERY GUEST who leaves one of our restaurants will come away with a firm impression of the place. Of course, food will be a major factor, as will the greeting they received, the scope of the menu, the ambience of the dining room—even the cleanliness of the restroom. But no one factor is as singularly important as the performance of—

and the guest's connection with—their server. In many ways, servers are the face, voice and calling card of our business. The importance of their role cannot be overestimated.

Servers are not made; they're born. I can train any smart, hard-working person in all of our systems, give them support and knowledge and use all of my resources to prepare them to excel. But if they don't have the hospitality gene, they just won't cut it.

A Venn diagram showing the qualities of a good server would show a million circles illustrating the wide variety of individuals who can do this job well, but they would all connect in the middle at one common point defined by a few simple qualities: friendly, happy, flexible, attentive, anticipatory, sincere and most importantly, desirous to please. There are a few more words I could throw in there, but I think you get the point. A good server truly must want to serve people, to take care of their every need at the table. If you do not personally share this combination of qualities—and let's face it, most of us veer toward the selfish and may consider some of these qualities demeaning—it's probably hard to understand those who embrace them.

One thing a server is *not*—and I cannot stress this enough—is a servant. For too many years that seemed to be the prevailing sensibility. I am still amazed—frankly, disgusted—by the manner in which some guests treat service staff. Snapping their fingers, yelling out, blaming servers for things out of their control and worse, depriving them of their gratuity as punishment for something they did not do. (I'll discuss tipping in detail later.) Every guest rightfully has certain expectations of the service staff, including that they be pleasant, knowledgeable, accurate, efficient and attentive. I myself expect *at least* those things from my staff. But please do not think that a server is at your beck and call. On a busy night he or she is likely to have forty-nine more guests at any given moment that require the same level of service that you, their fiftieth guest, require.

As I mentioned earlier, at my core, I am a server. Yes, I also own the business, and no, I do not take a regular shift each night. But I came up in this industry as a server in a random job as a bored teenager. It exposed me to the profession, and in a deeper sense, exposed the person I was meant to become. I embraced it from the beginning, and to this day it remains my favorite part of the job. So I know what it means to be a server. In fact, it means many different things. We may be a psychologist, mathematician, savant, architect, friend, confidant, laugher at bad jokes, crisis manager, babysitter, acrobat and much more. For some high-maintenance guests, we may need to play all of these roles within the course of ninety minutes.

I walk into one of our restaurants, glance around and see one server helping a toddler color between the lines of a coloring book, another memorizing every single item that a group of ten is ordering (including special requirements), another laughing sincerely at a lame joke from the table of six business colleagues and another pouring wine and listening sympathetically while a young couple laments their future in-laws meddling in the planning of *their* wedding. You can bet that each of those actions comes from a place of genuine concern, not from a rote training script or, cynically, a desire to extract the biggest tip.

Every once in a while we hire someone who doesn't work out. Not every good server is as good in one setting as they are in another. When our managers set out to hire service staff, they look first for the basic qualities I mentioned above, and second for the qualities that match their particular restaurant's needs. As with everything else in this business, there is no one-size-fits-all solution.

During one management meeting, we singled out the best server at Amis, our Roman trattoria neighborhood joint, and discussed the possibility of moving her to Vetri. At the end of the day, we realized that her excellence in Amis's fast-casual setting likely would not translate to the more refined setting of Vetri. She is a real mover and shaker—literally. The guests at Amis love her energy. In contrast, we would probably come to the same conclusion with the top servers at Vetri—that they wouldn't quite cut it at Amis. While servers at Vetri generally need to comport themselves like ballet dancers, those at Amis may be better off tapping into their inner rock star. The loud music, loud guests and faster pace of Amis call for a whole different skill set than the more serene setting of Vetri.

We vigorously train our staff to uphold a set of common service guidelines in addition to the specifics unique to each place. Always greet guests with a smile on their way in and wish them well on their way out. Always sincerely thank a guest for joining us—even those who may have voiced some concerns. Be polished and well-spoken. Be friendly but unobtrusive. Never say "no" without offering an alternative. The list goes on, but the main point is that no server should simply memorize these guidelines and regurgitate them robotically. Natural-born hospitality pros infuse them with their own personality and sincere desire to provide joy.

We have to give each server latitude if we expect their personality to shine. Because they do wear many hats, they need the confidence to determine which one is required at any given moment and to try it on for size.

One such hat is Nutritionist. Servers walk a fine line when a guest asks for nutritional information about our food, especially when they add comments about their own weight or the diet that they're on. Ours is a job of pleasing guests, but we are obliged to find out whether someone sincerely needs to watch what they eat, or if they're just trying to feel good about their order. On a recent vacation, my wife, who is generally nutrition-minded, was faced with the choice of a side green salad or fresh-cut French fries. She looked at the server with a smile in her eye.

"Now, really, how many people opt for the salad?" she asked.

The server had yet to determine my wife's goal, and politely replied, "Some people do. It's pretty split, actually."

"Well, we're on vacation, and calories don't count on vacation, right?"

Starting to get it, the server replied, "Of course not. We actually remove them in the kitchen!" He leaned in a bit, and offered the coup de grâce. "And the reality is, most people *don't* get the salad!"

When a guest has genuine concerns about food, we do take it very seriously. Any sensitivity regarding allergies, religious preferences and specific health issues is addressed with respect. And when guests don't expressly offer their thoughts on the matter, we try to understand their true goals. Are you on a strict diet or are we just being sensible tonight? Can I offer dessert or should I suggest a table share? I wouldn't want to be responsible for your inability to stay in shape! But I can't let you leave without having the housemade gelato—it's the lowest-fat dessert we offer.

Donning the Psychologist hat can extend far beyond the typical scenario of the bartender propping up the downtrodden bar patron. It often takes some effort to figure out exactly what a guest needs, let alone what they really want. The fact that every server must read every guest already takes a fair amount of behavioral analysis. Does a frown indicate dismay with the ambience, their table or a service mishap? Or did they arrive with that frown due to traffic or a quarrel with the partner they're now about to share a meal with in a public place? We can help with all of that, and you'd be surprised how often we do.

While we don't invade anyone's personal life, we do look for body-language cues, a deviation from ordering habits by regulars, multiple absences from the table for phone calls and so on. We have seen it all, so nothing will be a surprise. Rest assured that we are constantly on the lookout for such incidents. It's part of our training, but also just a natural quality of being a server.

One time, a couple was clearly engaged in an argument as they arrived at our restaurant. Their server and I both noticed the tension and quickly acknowledged each other's perception, so we were prepared for anything that might come next.

They sat down and ordered a bottle of wine and three courses. Fortunately, their argument wasn't loud or even very noticeable to others. Everything was a muted debate, starting with the wine order.

"I don't care; just order something."

"Fine. White or red?"

"I just said I don't care. Didn't you hear me, or are you just not listening as usual?"

Midway through appetizers, the woman stormed out of the restaurant and service threatened to grind to a halt. What did we do? Well, we couldn't ignore it; that would show a complete lack of awareness and concern on our part.

Diplomatically, the server approached the table.

"Will the lady be returning?"

The man chuckled and said, "Oh, I'm pretty sure she won't be."

"That's fine, sir. Should I wrap up the rest of your food?"

"Of course not! I'm still here. I'll eat it all, no problem."

Oddly, he began to smile and looked happy as he ate his way through three courses. He finished the wine, then had dessert and coffee. His reaction dictated our reaction, and despite the unfortunate earlier tension,we managed to contain it so the other guests were mostly oblivious while he remained comfortable with his choice to stay.

For servers, it's all about complementing the energy put forth by the table itself. We've got to be prepared to downshift and upshift within just a few steps. While one table may be filled with a celebratory group, the next table could be somberly remembering a friend whose memorial service they just attended.

Acrobat is one of the roles of server that draws frequent comment. "How in the world do you carry all those plates of hot food in one hand above your head through a roomful of people and a maze of tables and chairs?" All I can say about this one—from personal experience—is that you live it and you learn it. Just like baseball players, servers make errors in the field of play. We forget orders, bring plates to the wrong table, omit a special request and sometimes drop things in the middle of the dining room. As with all such mistakes, it's not the action but the reaction that matters.

One forgettable moment of my career was when I was a server at the country club in Long Island. I had a table of ten who lingered longer than we would have preferred.

Trying to gain back a couple of minutes so we could seat the next party, I decided to try to fit every plate, bowl, glass and piece of silverware on a single bus tray and clear the whole table in one fell swoop. Fast forward about three seconds, and probably the loudest crash I have ever heard in a restaurant dining room stopped the room cold.

As I lay on the floor amid broken glass and shards of china, the chef, straight out of central casting with an enraged face and a meat cleaver in his hand, ran out of the kitchen, stood over me, surveyed the debris and shouted, "Benjamin! We *reuse* those, you know!"

It wasn't the best or most proper reaction, but it did draw a few chuckles from guests. I rose to my feet, started clearing the floor and swept the scene as quickly and quietly as I could.

As an owner and, at times, manager, I've been in that chef's shoes myself more than once. But I've learned—and I always drive this home to my staff—that the spectacle that occurs after the accident is what makes guests most uncomfortable. You don't want everyone running around with brooms and dustpans and endless apologies to nearby guests. One brief apology will suffice, along with one or two staff quickly clearing the area while the rest go about their business. A little humor never hurts, either. Once when a server dropped some expensive plates with a loud crash, a regular customer glanced over to me while the server quietly cleaned up the mess.

"There goes this week's payroll," he said with a smile.

Smiling back, I said, "Don't worry, I'll just add it to your bill!"

Whether it's a resoundingly broken glass or a chicken dish mistaken for fish, most guests reserve their reaction until they see ours. And we're grateful that good people are quick to forgive those who carry themselves with professionalism and self-respect.

Which leads me to my last point about what makes a server. Waiting tables in a good restaurant is no longer viewed as a stopgap or stepping stone to a better career. It's a job with dignity that requires special gifts and abilities, a full and viable career in itself. That's why it always bugs me when I get the inevitable phone call every May from one of my acquaintances.

"Hi Jeff, how ya doin'?"

"Great, and you? How's the summer shaping up for your family?"

"Actually, that's why I'm calling. You know my daughter, the junior in college?"

"Oh absolutely. A junior already? Wow! I remember that when

you first came in she was in elementary school. How is she making out? Any plans for the future?"

"Well, she still has a year to figure it out and there are lots of possibilities, but she wanted to take it easy this summer since next year it'll be all about preparing for her career."

"Uh huh." I know what's coming next...

"I'm hoping you could use her for the summer on your staff. She gets home the first week of June and heads back right before Labor Day. Of course, we're going to be away for a couple of weeks on a family vacation, and we have the house down the shore that she'll be visiting, but other than that she really wants to work in one of your restaurants and is eager to get started. She's a real people person, so she can wait tables, host, whatever."

Yup, whatever.

Not that I blame him for asking. Historically in America we've viewed the service industry as a means to an end. How many times have we heard about the actor who survived in New York by picking up a shifts as a waiter or the attorney who paid for his law school tuition by bussing tables? Of course that still happens, but increasingly service staff, especially at the mid-casual level and above, can and do make a good career of it. Any restaurant that sets high service standards for its customers relies on service staff longevity to maintain those standards and is always looking for opportunities to promote based on achievement and incentive. Case in point: the opening server at Vetri in 1998 was yours truly!

Homegrown staff understand and can easily convey the mission of the organization, which is incredibly important. Over time they become part of the family—their successes are celebrated and their failures commiserated. So my answer to the guy who asks if we can give his daughter a job is a thoughtful one:

"I'm sure she would be great, but our training program is pretty intensive, and by the time she'd be ready to assume a position on the floor, summer will be virtually over. My apologies, but our current staff has preference of shift and we simply wouldn't be able to guarantee much work anyway."

Absent all diplomacy, it might be fun to reply, "Sure, no problem, just send her by whenever she's ready and we'll set her up as a full-on server. Come to think of it, my daughter is off for the summer, too, so can we do a switch kind of thing where she works in your law firm? She loves to argue; she does it every day. She would make a great lawyer. Maybe throw her a couple of the easier cases. What do you say?"

You get the point. Perhaps the formal study of restaurant service isn't as rigorous as in other careers, but the training is nonetheless long, hard work, and when it translates into top professional ability, a tremendous sense of accomplishment is earned. To those of us with careers in the service industry, that sense is refreshed daily by connecting with challenging guests and receiving compliments from our peers. Of course, on some days the sense of accomplishment comes by simply ending your day disaster-free.

The Tipping Point

When one server is successful, we're all achievers

BACK WHEN I WAS an undergrad studying hotel and restaurant management, still not exactly sure which end of the business I would wind up in, something happened in a restaurant one night that has stayed with me to this day. And the lesson learned gets right to the heart of our service philosophy at Vetri.

I was with my family at a typical steakhouse. The atmosphere was mid-casual, a place where you'd expect pretty good service. Halfway into the meal I realized my water glass was empty, and for several minutes I silently scanned the room hoping to flag down our server to ask him for a refill. My family noticed my dilemma and said the same things everyone says in that situation: "Where's your server when you need them?" "You should never be without water." "You shouldn't have to *ask* for a refill, let alone search for your server for *fifteen* minutes!"

Finally, a different server walked by and I politely stopped her.

"Would you mind refilling my water glass, please?" I asked, still thirsty but relieved that the wait would soon be over.

"Let me get your server," she said, never missing a step as she walked right by.

So much for the wait being over. I'd heard that line before, but it hit me right then, and hard: "Let me get your server" really means "Let me get the person you're paying and *they* can get you your water." Since she wasn't getting any of the tip from our table, she didn't feel responsible. It was the only possibility that made sense. Given the amount of time it would have taken for her to go find our server, and then for our server to finish what he's doing and come to our table with the water pitcher, it would have been easier for everyone if she'd just handled the refills herself.

Thus, "Let me get your server" became one of the lines that led me into this business and helped form my definition of service. Over the years, I've heard it so many times it's become an inside joke to my family. Sometimes when we're in a new restaurant, I'll wait until our server is out of sight and ask a different server to provide something for our table, just to see what they say. Whenever we hear, "Yes, sure," we expect to be well taken care of. But when the reply is, "Let me get your server," we know what's in store for the rest of the meal, and it's usually mediocrity.

Of course, not every restaurant that uses the traditional tipping system—where each server gets all tips from their own tables—has service like that college-town steakhouse. At our restaurants, we prefer a different way.

Early on, at Vetri, we set up a tip-pooling system where guests' gratuities are combined at the end of the night and split by the service staff. All of our restaurants have a similar system, as do some of our colleagues'. It's really just one incentive, part of the larger goal of creating a successful environment where everyone feels invested in their job and their place in the family. You don't have to be in the tipping pool to lend your hand wherever it's needed. The sense of teamwork extends from owners to managers to the back of the house. Any staff member will give any guest a hand whenever they ask. Believe me, every hand is needed every night.

Anyone who's eaten in a restaurant, let alone worked in one, knows how hectic it can get: two to three hours of nonstop running, every night of the week (if we're lucky). So many different circumstances that can quickly create chaos vary so much that it's impossible to prepare for everything. At any given moment, some random series of events in one server's station can toss them into a tailspin, and they can only get by with a little help from their friends. We can train and practice and prepare all we want, but once service starts, it's all hands on deck.

Here's a scenario that could happen to the best of servers. Let's say Jon's station has three tables, and two of them from the first seating stayed ten minutes longer than planned. The two new parties that just replaced them—including one group of ten—remain somewhat peeved that they had to wait. Meanwhile, the third table from the first seating is *still* lingering over coffee while their replacements simmer impatiently at the bar. Already the pressure is on Jon to win back the confidence of all three second-seating parties.

After greeting the ten-top, he takes their drinks order and hands them the wine list. Moving to the next table, a couple on their first date, he sees they're both so nervous that they can't decide what to order, so they tag-team him with questions about every dish. One is vegetarian and wants a recitation of ingredients in each menu item along with potential swaps. As Jon describes the eleventh dish to them, he notices a few eyeballs from the big group glancing his way, apparently ready to order wine. Meanwhile, he knows he's got to spend a few seconds at the third table to make sure there are no more coffee refills, and if there are not, he will gently drop the check as a subtle hint that it's time to leave, along with the message, "Whenever you're ready…"

At this point, another server may notice Jon's dilemma and step in to take the lucrative wine order while Jon finishes his dramatic reading of the menu to the couple. The watchful manager will continue to chat with the group at the bar waiting to be seated to ease their tension, and once the lingering group does exit, the nearest hands will begin prepping that table for the turn. No single person is solely responsible for any particular table or guest or job. Many patrons are under the impression that their server is the only person who can help them, and they may not ask anyone else. That can lead to frustration when they need something while their server is trying to deliver ten entrées from the kitchen to another table. In a well-run restaurant, guests need not be so timid. Just ask the next server you see to get you what you need; they're there for you as much as your primary server is.

Sometimes I'll notice that one host is seating a table while the other is helping to reset another, and there's nobody at the front door. So naturally, I'll stand there and greet customers until one of the hosts returns. At the end of the day, when one person steps up to help another, it's not done to seek the spotlight. We just do our best as a group to help make the guests shine.

Inside the Staff Meeting

We're all in this together. So let's eat!

ALL BUSINESSES HAVE meetings, and the restaurant business is no exception. On the corporate level, we have our weekly profit-and-loss (P&L) meetings to discuss revenue and expenses, with the predictable goals of raising one while lowering the other.

We also hold regular management meetings where the owner-ship group and managers of all our restaurants convene to address financials, staffing, best practices and more; we even reserve a portion of the meeting to discuss specific guests. Finally, we have nightly staff meetings in each restaurant—the most interesting of them all—which lead into the traditional "family meal" that kicks off each night of service.

I often read business books for exposure to new ideas and angles for growing the Vetri Family. One recent title that made an impression is *Death by Meeting*, by Patrick Lencioni. As the title suggests, there's a widespread belief in the corporate world that an excessive number of meetings curbs production and adds no value. But the real takeaway from that book is the notion that any meeting can be productive if it has direction and engages everyone in the room.

In our early days, meetings were more organic. We would realize we needed to figure something out, then quickly get together and just do it. As we've grown, we've had to make more effort to schedule meetings, but we try not to fall into the trap of having meetings for meetings' sake. We should all be smarter than that.

Our managers' meeting schedule is fairly regular, but the content—like the business itself—is so dynamic that it's almost impossible to set an agenda. We start off covering weekly financial performance, guest counts, cost containment and basic staff issues. But then it gets interesting. Each manager inevitably has something enlightening to say about certain guests who've visited in the last week, with the details offering insight for the other managers on how to replicate the good and avoid the bad.

Since I can't be in all of our restaurants all night every night, the managers' meeting is where I get to hear about the little things that worked—or didn't—so I can continuously shape our best practices as a group. One manager may say, "Hey, we tried this great happy hour special at Osteria that just killed. And it almost killed me, too! You know our happy hour goes from five to seven, right? Well, we ran out of arancini at 6:59! Close call, but very successful. Why don't you guys try it at your place next week?" Another might tell a cautionary tale. "For the last two weeks we tried to do scrapple at brunch and it did not go over well. So please, any of you who do brunch, *don't* do scrapple."

I love how productive and empowering these meetings can be, as each person is encouraged to jump in with comments, stories and suggestions. I could take notes beforehand and then address the group with all of this information myself. But running a meeting as a monologue, instead of the dialogues that typify ours, is the best way to lose your audience. Certain meetings do require me to do most of the talking, but at the end, like a baseball player after an out, I always throw it around the horn and let each person speak up. It's a no-holds-barred atmosphere and we get exactly the right kind—

and right amount—of input. As much as everyone is encouraged to pipe up, they're equally encouraged to simply pass the mic if they've got nothing productive to add. There's nothing more tedious than someone talking just for the sake of having talked. It's a waste of everyone's time and usually pretty transparent.

We do hold one meeting that you would be hard-pressed to find in any other industry—although it happens in every restaurant: the preshift meeting. By far it is the most important meeting at any restaurant, the equivalent of a sports team's pregame locker-room talk, packed with a detailed game plan and lots of energy and emotion. Before each shift, the manager gathers the entire service staff in the dining room, and often the back-of-house guys too, to talk about how the night will go and to elevate the energy level. It starts with getting key info on the table so everyone's on the same page.

"Here are the specials for the evening. Here are the things we ran out of last night that we weren't able to replace for tonight; make sure you inform each guest up front. Here are some wines that we are long on that we should probably try to move, but only when it works. The bar staff came up with this awesome new cocktail we need to share. And here is a company-wide announcement that you should be aware of." And so on. This part of the meeting can be a bit preachy, but with good managers, it's usually over in a flash. I've attended preshift meetings where a general manager will drone on, "Here are your specials… These are the VIPs who are coming in tonight… Here are the vegetables for the night… Have a great service." Like your worst high-school chemistry teacher, this stuff just puts everyone to sleep. But with great managers, once the key info is imparted, things start to get interesting.

"Okay, here we go. If you didn't know already, Jessie's girl just had a baby!" Applause and laughter among the staff. "He's not going to be in tonight, but we are so excited that Jill came in and is covering for him." High fives for Jill. "We got some really great VIPs coming tonight. David, you've got Charles Barkley around nine o'clock—make sure you save some energy for that!" David pretends to dunk a basketball and gets a chest-bump from the server next to him. "Now listen, this is really exciting... we've got *eighty* people coming in tonight who are first-time guests. You know what that means? Eighty future regulars! Let's wow them." Lots of looks around the room from one server to another, raising eyebrows and giving thumbs up—they're ready to make it happen. "Okay, so I just told you the specials that the kitchen has come up with; let's all have a taste so you'll know how to sell them." A tray comes out and in less than a minute the food disappears. "And hey, the big party at Table Six on the first turn, remember that those same guests were here last year on this same night for the same celebration. Let's make it extra special for them, okay?"

Then it's time to really break the ice. Unlike most businesses' staff meetings that feature all the same faces, the front of the house staff in a restaurant changes every single night. There are fourteen different shifts during the week, and since no one server works all of them, most shifts feature a different lineup. So from one night to the next, after we've gotten past the pertinent information, we like to build camaraderie and infuse energy in the hour just before we all get slammed. We'll play Trivial Pursuit or Jeopardy where all the answers and questions revolve around food in general or our restaurants and guests specifically. Sometimes we'll give out prizes—a piece of candy, or a gift certificate to one of our places or a colleague's restaurant. That's one way we get pumped up for service. Other nights we'll have a wine-tasting session with the sommelier or a quick beverage class, with each person getting a sip.

The preshift meeting will differ in its details, but it always delivers the same important message. "It's five o'clock, you're already enjoying yourself, so let's keep this vibe going until midnight. Let's go out there and kick some ass!"

All my friends in the business run their pre-shift meeting differently, but one common point is that it's always planned out. As loose as these meetings appear to be, they are always tightly woven beforehand. One of the stars of the pre-shift meeting, in my experience, is Bobby Stuckey at Frasca in Boulder, Colorado.

"Pre-service is the building block that sets up every evening,"

Bobby told me. "It gives us a chance to put the focus on hospitality and each guest's experience. Our GM and I come in early every day and meditate on pre-service so we can prepare an inspiring forty-five-minute meeting. Without it, we wouldn't be able to work on the mistakes we made the night before, or improve on the great things we did."

One of Bobby's tricks to creating the most impact is to hold the staff meeting during the portion of the day when everyone is at their most relaxed—the staff dinner, also known as the family meal.

Family meal is a long-standing tradition in the restaurant business, the one meeting that sets our industry apart from others. Just before service every night, usually right after the instructional staff meeting, everyone sits down together to eat, laugh, talk about the night and replenish their energy for the craziness ahead. Staff meals usually consist of something on the menu that night or a dish created out of excess ingredients. Lest you think it's mere food for afterthought, remember--it's prepared by some of the best chefs in the city.

The real point of staff meal is that it's shared with family, albeit one's work family. Let's sit around the table and have a conversation. Let's talk about work, or about life. It's always special when we break bread with those we're close to, and food, the one thing none of us can live without, turns out to be the best team-builder of all.

Eight Things Servers Should Know

Freshen up, don't pass the buck and learn where to draw the line

DINING EXCITES ALL SENSES—SMELL INCLUDED.

Be aware of the aromas in the room; we should only be smelling food and wine. If you just took a smoke break, ate a pickle or are wearing perfume, you're affecting the guests' sense of smell. That's why the fresh flowers on our tables are either unscented or very lightly scented.

GUESTS SHOULD BE THE ONLY ONES CHEWING.

Sure, I espouse fresh breath, but chomping and snapping gum in front of a guest is just rude, and one of the surest ways to annoy me.

RESPECT YOUR COLLEAGUES.

Most restaurant employees have basic respect for their coworkers, but what about the restaurant up the street? Never speak ill about your competitors. Who knows, you may work there some day. As long as we strive to be the best, there is plenty of room on the playing field.

TASTE IS A PERSONAL PREFERENCE.

Just because you don't care for artichokes doesn't mean that your guest won't. Telling a guest you don't like it doesn't do much for anyone. Feel free to point out a dish you like better, but, "Ew, not for me!" isn't a great way to represent the chef.

MISTAKES AREN'T HABITUAL.

Have you ever complained to a server only to hear, "Oh, that happens all the time"? What does that say about a restaurant? If it happens all the time and nobody has corrected it, it's probably a matter of time before the place is consistently empty. Sounds like a job for the expediter, not the guest.

DON'T LEAVE A JOB UNDONE.

A partially cleared table indicates to a guest that we appear to be ready to bring their next course or turn their table, but we are preventing this from actually happening. It also tells a diner that they (a) eat too slowly and/or (b) eat too much. A table of four with just one person eating and three with an empty space in front of them is awkward for everyone. Wait till they're all done, and then clear. You wouldn't partially *serve* them, would you?

FRIENDLY VS FRIEND—KNOW THE DIFFERENCE.

Know your guest and know their boundaries. Being friendly with every diner is encouraged, but making friends with all of them isn't going to happen. Pretending every guest is your best buddy is disingenuous at best and can lead to great discomfort.

DON'T PASS THE BUCK.

"Let me get your server" is a phrase that makes my skin crawl. You may as well say "I have absolutely no desire to help you because you aren't in my station and I don't get your tip." Give a little help whenever and wherever it's needed; you will have the favor returned, I assure you.

PART FIVE

BE OUR GUESTS

"You have 135 seats, right?"
"Yes, we do."
"So how can you not seat eighteen at once?"

One Size Does Not Fit All

Every first-time diner is a potential future regular

I LIVE FOR CUSTOMER SERVICE. It's always on my mind, no matter what side of the transaction I'm on. I think about it when I'm shopping for clothes in a retail store, buying a car at a dealership or dealing with a utility company on the phone. I also have the pleasure of being a customer service agent and relish the opportunity to practice what I preach. The expectations I have of others when I am a customer are the same ones we strive to meet or exceed as a staff every night.

I've realized that what sets the guest-service superstars apart is the fact that they don't need to work at it. To them, superior customer service comes naturally. Dare I say, they are simply nice people.

If all you want to do is make the killing—get in, get out, get your money—then by all means size up your guest and let your first impression be the only one you act upon. Worse yet, treat everyone exactly the same. But if you want to create a sustainable, profitable business, you need to establish relationships, not customers.

The trick is to enter every situation with the thought that this is a two-way interaction, not a one-sided action to be played by the book. How I start the interaction goes a long way toward informing how the other person will respond and ultimately sets the tone for the guest's satisfaction.

We always say we can get someone to eat in our restaurants once. That's easy. But can we get them to repeat? That's the challenge. Each day at our preservice meeting we review the guest list with our staff. Our Open Table account indicates "First-Time Diner"—or as we call them, future regulars. Every regular was once a first-time diner. The question is, what did we do to bring them back? Was it the food? Did they receive exceptional service? Did we meet a special request? Maybe all of the above. Certainly the cultivation of every repeat customer began the minute they decided to dine here. How were they treated on the confirmation phone call? Were they put on hold, and if so, for how long? Did they get the reservation they wanted, or did we have to offer alternatives? Are they coming in for a special occasion, and what can we do to make it more special? Can we accommodate a request for a particular table? Whatever the specific need, the more notes we seek and the customer provides, the better we can prepare to serve them and the fewer surprises when they arrive.

All this information positions our service staff to appropriately address each guest on arrival. Nothing disappoints me more than the one-size-fits-all method of guest service seen in corporate restaurants. The guy on the first date and the team of business associates are in the restaurant for different reasons and require very different interactions. It is up to us to make sure they both leave thinking they had exceptional service, but if they compared notes, they would not have had the same experience.

I do understand the need for standard practices; training would be a nightmare if we simply told staff, "Approach the guest and figure out a way to get them what they need." But when you hire the right people and create a nurturing environment for them, you don't need to create a script that allows for no deviation. The minute you tell your staff there is no room for authentic interaction is the minute you guarantee failure when the inevitable deviation occurs. Because that's when they stop approaching each customer with an open mind.

Of course, certain customers can really test your commitment to maintain that open mind right from the start. I have struggled with this challenge myself at times. During Vetri's first year, I took a call one Friday afternoon from a woman requesting a reservation that night for her boss. We weren't very busy during the week at this point, but Fridays were booked months in advance. We only had thirty-five seats, so it didn't take much to fill up, but that also left us no room to hold back a "just in case" table to accommodate last-minute guests.

I informed the woman that we were full. "But my boss *really* wants to come," she said. "Isn't there something you can do?"

She was very pleasant, and I sincerely wanted to help, but I just couldn't do it and made that clear with a sense of finality.

She didn't give up. "What if I told you he was the president of a multinational pharmaceutical company?"

I replied, "Ma'am, I would love to accommodate your boss, no matter what his position, but we are so small that last-minute reservations are very difficult. However, I will call you back if we get a cancellation."

Sure enough, an hour later a deuce cancelled, so I called her. She thanked me up and down and assured me her boss would be there. That night, a man and a woman walked in wearing jeans and casual jackets and mentioned the name on the reservation. Displaying no body language to reveal my suspicion—at least I hoped not—I seated the table and walked back into the kitchen.

I complained to Marc, "That guy whose assistant called just showed up. Look at him, he ain't the president of anything!" Marc just glanced at him and said, "Well, whoever he is, he's about to eat real well, so hopefully he enjoys it."

My annoyance wasn't caused by the fact that this guy didn't seem to be president material, but because I believed his assistant had lied to me to get him in.

I approached the table and greeted the couple again, curious to see where this would go. After a brief exchange, the man asked about wine, and from there my first impression took a sharp turn. We ended up having a spirited conversation about wine and discovered that we were both enamored with the Quintarelli label, swapping stories about recent bottles we'd enjoyed. We continued to talk through the evening, and the couple really enjoyed their time with us. Toward the end of the meal the man asked to meet Marc, and said, "You know, he contributed a recipe to our company cookbook for diabetics and I wanted to thank him." He reached in his wallet and handed me his business card. Sure enough, he was the president of a major pharmaceutical company.

We've enjoyed many more meals together, hosted his wedding dinner and since his retirement we've flown to the West Coast to cook at his house. He's become a true friend, thanks to the commitment we made early on to approach each first-time customer with an open mind, with the hope that they might become future regulars.

The Educator

"I see four empty tables. Why can't we just sit there? Or there?"

ONE OF MY EARLY management positions was running the dining facilities of DLJ investment bank in New York City. Back in the '80s and '90s, many banks provided a heavily subsidized cafeteria so that employees could eat lunch on site and get back to their desks faster, thereby increasing profits. The onus was on my staff to create such a high-quality experience that the choice would be a no-brainer. One of my favorite things about the job was the opportunity to interact with the same guests. The more I saw familiar faces, the more I realized that we were successfully threading the needle between efficiency and quality.

It was at the DLJ cafeteria that I first met "the Educator."

The hospitality business is both blessed and cursed by the fact that most people have eaten at a restaurant many times and have a basic understanding of what works and what doesn't. Not many industries can boast (or lament) such an experienced customer base, and that base of knowledge usually helps service run smoothly. But there is a small subset of restaurant-goers who believe they've earned the right to offer advice to our staff on the spot, and then later to let the rest of the world know what *should* have been done via Yelp or other online forums. I call this guest the Educator.

It was my second day on the job at DLJ, and I had made my rounds to the various executive dining rooms and special-events spaces. The rest of my afternoon would be spent in the cafeteria monitoring the flow of service to see where I could make an impact. I was standing in the middle of the cafeteria talking to the chef, Billy, when he stopped in midsentence and said, "Uh, gotta run. See you later," and disappeared into the kitchen. At the same moment one of the bank analysts entered the cafeteria and proceeded to walk around the serving area taking stock of the day's offerings.

Occasionally he nodded his head; once in a while he smiled, but more often he frowned. Since he was alone and had a concerned look on his face, I decided to approach.

"Excuse me, sir. Hello. Is there something I can help you with?"

"No, not really, just looking." Pause. Stare. "Who are you?" he finally said.

I introduced myself and encouraged him to ask me for anything he needed. He shook my hand, introduced himself as Steve, and said flatly, "You should add another soup station."

"Excuse me?"

"Another soup station. You have only one and I'm in a hurry and really don't have time to wait, but I like soup, so you should have another soup station to handle the flow."

"That's a great idea." I took out my little notepad and jotted down his suggestion. "I'll check with corporate and see where we can put it."

"No, you won't."

"Excuse me?" I repeated, taken aback.

"I've mentioned it before and it never gets done. I'm just telling you because you should do it, but you won't."

Well, I like a challenge, and I love when I can accommodate a guest, especially with something so easy. I silently vowed that the very next day there would be two soup stations up and running, and I would wait for him to arrive. I'd show him!

That evening as I was taking inventory of our smallwares I noticed two soup serving crocks in their original packaging. I smiled broadly, cleaned them and installed them on the opposite side of the original soup station.

At lunch the following day I was standing with the chef once again when he abruptly excused himself to the kitchen. There was Steven entering the room. I hightailed it over to him.

"Steven! Follow me, I have your soup station all set up! No more waiting!"

He did follow me, but what didn't follow was the expected smile or show of gratitude for delivering on my promise. Instead he looked at the soup, ladled himself a cup, put the lid on it and said dismissively, "You need a wider selection in the salad bar."

Thus began my relationship with the Educator. He would follow me throughout my career, providing plenty of interesting situations, confrontations and conundrums.

There was that time, two weeks after we opened Vetri, when the Educator came in with an extra guest beyond his expected party of two. Although we had a deuce already prepared for him, he knew exactly what we needed to do instead.

"Take that chair from that table over there, turn our table forty-five degrees and you've just added a seat for my extra guest."

Never mind that the extra chair would have sat directly in the path of the servers, or that the newly angled table would encroach on guests at the adjacent table. None of those facts mattered to the Educator, because he only has the immediate issue at hand. For him, solutions exist in a vacuum and to add any other variables—regardless of how obvious their impact would be—completely upsets his apple cart and causes him to school you on how "the customer is always right."

Another time, she (the Educator comes in both sexes) showed up early on a booked-solid Saturday night without a reservation, but with a solution already in hand.

"Oh great," she said upon entering, "you clearly aren't full tonight, so we will just sit over there."

While our thirty-five-seat dining room was not yet full, the evening had just gotten underway and there was a very good reason for the apparent vacancy. When we take reservations, we specifically plan to seat one-third of the room first, and then the second third a half hour later and the final third a half hour after that. And as the first third of tables becomes open, we begin reseating the entire room. An hour after opening, we're packed, and it stays like that throughout the evening. This cycling method assures that we do not overburden the servers, the kitchen and most of all the guests. It's actually quite simple, and should be easy for anyone to grasp. So I tried to explain.

"I'm sorry ma'am, we actually do have that table reserved. Unfortunately, we are fully committed this evening. But we occasionally have no-shows, and some guests may eat and depart quicker than we expected. We'd be happy to seat you at that point if you'd like to come back."

"But you have four empty tables right now. Why can't we just sit there? Or there? Or there?"

"Within the next half hour, all of those tables will be filled by guests with reservations, so I need to have the tables ready for them."

That should do it, I thought. Clear as a bell.

"They aren't here now, though, so seat us now and we will be done by the time they get here."

"Ma'am, I certainly wish that were true, but we will not be able to adequately serve you in that amount of time."

"You mean you don't have faith in your ability? You should have stronger faith in yourselves if you are going to run a business."

"That isn't what I meant, ma'am," I replied, keeping my composure. "I was simply suggesting that a meal here often takes ninety minutes, and we wouldn't want you to be underwhelmed. Likewise, if you had a reservation, we would want your table ready at the time you reserved it so that you can be seated upon arrival. We owe that to all of our guests."

Now we should be all set, right?

"Come on, honey," she said brusquely, turning to her husband. "They clearly prefer an empty restaurant to having us here. Let's go. They'll be out of business in a month."

Even worse is when the Educator makes a reservation for a large party during the busiest times of the year—Christmas, graduation season, Mother's Day—along with making a generous offer to help us reconfigure the reservation book. The goal at hand? Fit their party into the main dining room to avoid the cost of booking one of our private spaces reserved for large groups.

Our largest restaurant has 135 seats in the main dining room, plus two private dining areas that seat thirty-two and sixty-five people, respectively. When they aren't booked, we open these private spaces for a la carte dining. But when they are booked privately by a large group, the rooms carry a minimum charge, for obvious reasons.

If space was the only factor, of course we could put as many seats together in the main dining room as it could hold. But space is not a factor—not at all. The factors we do consider include other guests' ability to enjoy themselves without being distracted by a large group; maintaining ample oven space to avoid delays in serving food; and ensuring that servers are able to meet every guest's expectations with equal attentiveness and speed.

Most of our guests who call with large-group reservations do not need to be given this information. The conversation usually goes something like this:

"Hello, I'd like to make a reservation for a party of eighteen on May 18."

"Certainly. Let me put you in touch with the catering department. They handle all reservations larger than twelve. Please hold for a moment."

"Thank you."

But when you're dealing with the Educator, it usually goes something like this:

"Hello, I'd like to make a reservation for a party of eighteen on May 18."

"Certainly. Let me put you in touch with the catering department. They handle all reservations larger than twelve. Please hold for a moment."

"Thank you."

All settled, right? Not so fast. Typically some period of time will elapse—it can be as short as a few minutes or as long as a day or two—before I hear back from the slightly annoyed Educator.

"Hello, I was hoping to book a table for eighteen on May 18." "Yes sir, I will transfer you to catering; they handle all parties larger than twel—"

"No, do not transfer me there. You already did that. That is not what I wanted. I just need a reservation. They want $3,000 just to have the room."

"I understand, sir. I would love to help you, but parties larger than twelve cannot be booked à la carte."

"Okay, so book me three tables of six."

"Sir, that is still eighteen people who will show up at the same time, expect to sit together and be served at the same time. But for several reasons, we are just not able to do it."

"You have 135 seats, right?"

"Yes, we do."

"So how can you not seat eighteen at once?"

"We can seat eighteen people in unrelated groups within the same general time period, but not eighteen people who all want to be seated at the same time and to receive their food at the same time."

"What difference does that make?"

At this point, it's clear that the Educator is not looking to learn or understand. No matter how the reservationist replies, one of two things will happen next.

Typically I will receive a message informing me that our reservationist was rude and explaining the basics of good customer service to me. I will hear about how important the occasion is for his child and family, and how they want more than anything to celebrate with us. And I will be asked, again, "So what are you going to do for me?" In these cases I apologize if any of our staff came off as rude, and gently explain how stressful it is to try to accommodate all the graduates and their families and that they sincerely do their best to accomplish this. Typically I never hear back.

On rare occasions, the Educator will spend a few minutes logging in as different users on Open Table to book those three tables of six. When the night comes and his party arrives after a beautiful graduation ceremony, the Educator will not have informed his guests that there are actually three different reservations and three different tables—and more importantly, that the restaurant has no idea they're together.

Invariably, Ed is the last to arrive; meanwhile grandma and grandpa are seated at a six top with quizzical looks on their faces wondering who isn't coming. Ed shows up loaded for bear and places the blame on a restaurant screw-up. The eager manager on the floor doesn't want a scene during graduation weekend, so she does her best to seat them all as close as possible. Ed receives stellar service, although now that his kid has graduated, he will never be back. Meanwhile, the tables around him may have waited a bit longer for their service.

Some Educators never learn.

Don't Let Them Get Your Goat

Sometimes a disgruntled customer just needs closure

THE AREA comprising the Lombardia and Piemonte regions in northern Italy, just south of the Alps, is known for its osso buco and deeply flavored game, as well as its preference for polenta over pasta and butter over olive oil.

It's also where Marc spent his apprenticeship as a young chef, immersed in the culture of food and wine that consumes every aspect of life. Today we travel through the area regularly, to see old friends and seek new insights and inspiration.

In the early days of Vetri, we were hailed as innovators for bringing northern Italian dishes that most diners were unfamiliar with to the New World. And while most of our customers were excited to taste authentic dishes and to learn about new ingredients, a few couldn't get around their preconceived notion of Italian food.

One evening two couples were dining together and, if you asked me, they were lucky to be there that night. Among other specials, we were serving spinach gnocchi—our most popular item both then and now—and for the main course, slow-roasted baby goat. It's a beloved dish in northern Italy, but many Americans are turned off by the mere suggestion of goat. They'll eat lamb without a second thought, not realizing it has a much gamier flavor. Goat has a subtle taste, and the way we prepared it—roasted for five hours then simmered in milk, with skin crisped just before service—brought out the best possible flavor and texture. We served it over a bed of soft polenta, which is very traditional.

Our spinach gnocchi also deserves some explanation. While most people think of gnocchi as starchy little dumplings, spinach gnocchi was our take, and considering that the word "gnocchi" means "round and plump," the name makes sense. We were proud to serve these ethereally light balls of spinach bound with a little ricotta and finished with brown butter, and most customers were happy to make them disappear.

Halfway through their meal, I noticed that the two couples were not thrilled with their experience. More than half of the food remained uneaten when their plates were returned to the kitchen between courses. Maybe they were frustrated by the service style; maybe it was the food. Whatever the problem, I was going to find out and fix it.

I checked in to ask if they were enjoying their meal. The most vocal of the group spoke up immediately.

"You know," she said, "we just don't get it."

"I'm sorry?" I asked and leaned forward, my interest piqued.

"Well, we come to an Italian restaurant and we get gnocchi that isn't like anything we've ever had before. I mean, who puts spinach in gnocchi? And there was no sauce on it. Gnocchi always comes with tomato sauce; instead it's covered in butter."

I explained how our dish was conceived, and assured them that similar versions of gnocchi are enjoyed throughout northern Italy. I suspected I wasn't getting through to them, and the vocal woman confirmed my concern.

"Well, it really wasn't that good."

I stood there thinking, *wow, they just trashed one of our best dishes. But that's okay, we'll just thrill them with our main course. It's time to send out the goat.*

Soon after the main dish was served, I went to check on them again. By now, I had taken over service for their table and made it my goal to educate and impress these people. If they were not going to be happy, I wanted it to be my fault. My heart sank when I noticed none of them were eating the goat.

"We won't even touch it," the woman said. "It's goat. Who eats goat? This is ridiculous."

"I'm sorry you feel that way," I said. "Slow-roasted goat is one of our very best dishes. It's traditional northern Italian, and I hoped you would enjoy it." I spoke a bit more about the origin of the recipe, but to no avail. Finally I caved and asked, "Can we prepare something else for you?"

We brought them a few other dishes, and I checked in with them several times during the meal. Mostly I tried to explain the wonderful variety of regional Italian cuisines that existed beyond spaghetti and tomato sauce.

"Think about it this way," I said, hoping to clarify via analogy. "If an Italian man visited the United States several times but only went to Maine, he'd go back to Italy and say, 'Everybody in America eats lobster.' And if his friend visited America just as frequently but only went to Texas, he would say, 'Everybody in America eats barbecue.'"

Hopefully I had expanded their horizons, and they seemed okay with my explanations. At the end of the meal, they thanked me for the extra attention.

A few days later I received a two-page letter from the spokes-woman. She noted how disappointed she had been with her meal, and reassured me that none of the dishes were Italian because, after all, she's Italian and her family had never served goat, and she thought it reprehensible that I had tried to convince her otherwise.

She closed by stating that she did not send the letter seeking anything in exchange. Rather, because of the cost she paid for the meal and because she was so upset when she left, she needed closure.

That last line really got me. I've heard "closure" used by people who have faced major losses in life, but never in reference to a disappointing meal. Knowing now that I should have left it at that, at the time I was just a brash young man and felt that I needed to educate this woman.

So I grabbed a review by a respected food writer who had expert knowledge of ethnic food and noted that her favorite dish at Vetri is the goat because it reminded her of travels through northern Italy. I copied it, along with other articles about roasted goat in Italy, and sat down to write a reply, mentioning that I truly enjoyed getting to know them, honestly thought I had addressed all their concerns and really wished they would have let me know they still weren't happy before they left. I added that it was important for her to know that what we served was identified as Italian food in most circles and that we did deliver exactly what we set out to serve her. Then I sealed the envelope and mailed it off to her.

From the moment I dropped it in the mailbox—until today, in fact—I was the one who needed closure!

I'm not impressed with myself for having sent that letter. It was argumentative and clearly something that should not have been sent. The customer isn't always right, but will always have their own perspective, and they are entitled to it. On that night we did not deliver what they believed we would.

The forty-five-year-old Jeff Benjamin would never have sent that letter. The twenty-nine-year-old Jeff Benjamin felt it was his duty to educate that customer.

I sometimes think about her, though I certainly never saw her again, and she didn't respond to my letter. And while I hope that she did get closure, I know that my own closure rests in the fact that I learned a valuable lesson that night and have yet to repeat that mistake.

Guests These Days

Ma'am, is that a wineglass in your handbag?

IMAGINE DINING AT a fine restaurant in the mid-1970s: white tablecloths, tuxedoed waiters, suit and tie for the man, fancy dress for the woman and a museum-like atmosphere in the dining room. The sommelier would be an older gentleman with a French accent, and the menu would be printed on oversized thick stock in cursive calligraphy inside a leather portfolio. There would be a delicate din comprising lightly clinking glasses, plates and silverware, and all of the guests would be engaged in muted conversations meant to stay within earshot of their table. The whole scene looks like a cartoon from the *New Yorker*.

Fast-forward to now, where the linen might be replaced by an uncovered farm table or something made of brushed steel. The wait staff, still professional, are no longer dressed like penguins. There's a lively buzz about the room and you may have to pay a bit more attention to hear your companion. The sommelier has a fifty-fifty chance of being female and often, very young. The menu, if there is one, has a whimsical font and design, or, in the case of Vetri, is handwritten.

The world changed when casual Friday began in the dot-com offices of the late 1990s, and when J. P. Morgan made it official policy in 2000, all others followed. Casual Friday became casual every day. But while dress code relaxed, our guests' level of interest and knowledge grew. Generally speaking, restaurant goers are worldlier than ever thanks to the ease of international travel and, of course, the Internet. As their perception of the restaurant experience changed, we changed along with it, from food to décor to service style. This new familiarity with formerly esoteric foods has opened up new possibilities for restaurateurs, but it's also raised the bar. We no longer get to introduce them to heirloom dishes and traditional cooking techniques. Instead, savvy diners arrive knowing what to expect, so the only surprise left is for us to deliver perfect execution.

But one thing hasn't changed. While most guests are so respectful and engaging that I would gladly welcome them into my own home, there are a handful who make you stop and say, "Hmm?" Like the guy who loudly brags about sexual conquests to his colleagues while seated near the young parents with their four-year-old daughter. Or the lusty couple who go beyond the occasional kiss to embarrass the older people nearby. Or the mother and father whose four-year-old daughter does cartwheels in the center of the dining room while they sit blithely eating instead of parenting. Far be it for some guests to curb their own enjoyment in any way in order to respect that of all the rest.

Anyone can lose their bearing for a moment and break the social contract. We understand. Just as the restaurant staff would like to be judged not by our mistakes but by corrective actions that follow, we give the same leniency. We do notice every word and action that crosses the line, but it's only when boorishness escalates that we step in and say something.

How do you let a group of strong-willed salesmen know that their enjoyment is causing a commotion without causing ill will? How can you let a parent know that their parenting style, which might be okay in the confines of their own home, is not acceptable in public? When people allow such behavior in the first place, odds are they think it's perfectly acceptable. So when we broach the topic, we try to be somewhat passive at first without sounding judgmental.

"Pardon me, folks, I notice your child is enjoying our dining room. I just wanted you to be aware that this aisle is a critical pathway for our staff and I'm concerned for her safety."

Ninety-nine percent of the time, the parents are apologetic. If it offends them, well, there's not much I can do. My goal is to ensure the comfort of all guests, so I'll err on the side of the lopsided majority every time.

"Gentleman, I'm so happy to see you having a great time together, but I hope that you keep the off-color comments to a minimum. We have mixed company in the room, including children. We appreciate your understanding and we hope you continue to enjoy yourselves."

Any time we admonish an unruly guest it's hit or miss, especially when you throw alcohol into the mix. Most people, a group of boisterous guys included, will take our cue and come back to civilization. But some—the ones that make you go "hmm?"—will actually double down and amp up their bad behavior. Their reaction is pretty typical, too.

"Hey, we're paying for this goddamn meal, we're out to have a good time and no one tells us what to do! We make the rules, pal."

Actually, *we* make the rules. And I'll let you in on a little secret. We have no problem going nuclear on a guest and ensuring that they'll never come back. It takes a lot to go there, and thankfully, I can count on one hand the number of times I've had to do so in my nearly twenty years in this business. But first, we use a few tricks to try to reel them in. Turns out, speaking softly to someone generally gets *them* to speak softly. It also calms them down and lets some air out of the pressure cooker. Try it sometime. Yell a command at someone and gauge the tone in the response. Then softly speak a suggestion and see how their tone mirrors yours.

One of our managers in particular, our beverage director Steve, has a gift for gently handling these situations. He's like the Jerk Whisperer. With a smile on his face and compassion in his tone, he has often approached an aggressive or drunken patron and simply suggested that this visit has ended. He will gently express our happiness in seeing that they had fun, and let them know that we look forward to having them come back as he slowly but surely allows them to decide it's time to leave. To date, he has a 100 percent success rate in defusing the most potentially disastrous situations.

In addition to those kinds of boorish behaviors, there's another level of questionable conduct that simply boggles the mind and yet, at the end of the day, is really harmless. A maître d' at one of the top restaurants in New York regaled me with the following tale over a glass of bourbon one night.

A couple in their mid-forties was having a pleasant meal, enjoying a nice bottle of wine and savoring the tasting menu. They had been engaging with the staff, sharing their opinions course by course. But the maître d' noticed that after each course, the gentleman had gotten up, walked to the restroom and returned after a good five minutes each time. By course five, the maître d' was worried that something might be wrong, and inquired, "Sir, is everything okay?"

"Why yes, everything is fine," the gentleman answered, somewhat taken aback.

The man let two courses go by without a visit to the restroom, but then, just before dessert, he made his fifth trip. Not wanting to create an uncomfortable situation, the maître d' simply waited to see the gentleman's demeanor upon returning. Noting that the man was smiling and nothing appeared to be out of the ordinary, he decided to chalk it up to a small bladder. Once the check was paid and the woman had gotten her coat, the guy made one last visit to the restroom. The maître d' stood in wait around the corner, and the instant the man exited the restroom, the maître d' stepped in to see if he could find any clues. It wasn't what he saw that solved the case, but what he didn't see. On the wall opposite the sink was an 11"x 17" empty white space that, at the beginning of the night, had been occupied by a framed painting of the Champs-Elysées.

The maître d' reentered the dining room, turned to see the gentleman heading for the door and noticed that his sport coat now had a boxy shape in the back with a dimension of approximately 11" x 17". To the maître d's credit, rather than make a scene, he hurried to the door to wish the couple well, and as he shook the gentleman's hand, he quietly said, "Sir, I neglected to put the price of the painting on your tab; should I just add it or send you a bill?"

Stunned, the man simply said, "Oh, uh, just go ahead and add it to the tab. Thank you." And the couple hurried off.

All you can do is shake your head at that kind of behavior and chalk it up to simple obliviousness. There was one time, though, that it hit a little closer to home.

The mother of a child in my daughter's dance class approached my wife one day to say what a great time she and her husband had at our new gastropub over the weekend. She rattled off all the food they ate and described several of the beers in detail. My wife was pleased and said, "Oh, you should let us know next time you are going. My husband loves when people we know come to his places and he'll be sure to spend some time at your table."

She thanked my wife, hesitated for a moment, then started to resume her story but with a sheepish grin. "I probably shouldn't tell you this," she laughed nervously, "but I will."

My wife grew nervous because she thought a complaint was coming. Instead, the woman continued, "We just loved the beer glasses so much that my husband sneaked a couple of them into the restroom, rinsed them off and stuck them in my purse. They had hundreds hanging from the bar rack, so we were sure they wouldn't miss two, right?"

Wrong. So wrong! How do you respond to someone who just

admitted to stealing from you and obviously doesn't see anything wrong with it? My wife just smiled and walked away. What she wanted to say was, "That's great. In fact, my husband is right now crawling through the window of your husband's office and taking his PC. He noticed that there are hundreds of PCs in the building, so I'm sure he won't miss it."

Eight Ways to Be a Desirable Customer

Show up, do unto others and don't steal the Sweet'N Low

DON'T STEAL.

No matter how small the item, it is factored into the cost. If you don't want increased prices, don't take it. That includes the Sweet'N Low!

DON'T BLAME THE MESSENGER.

Occasionally there are mishaps in a restaurant—we overcook an item, we leave off part of an order, we send the wrong dish, we spill something on a guest. Measure the restaurant on the corrective action taken rather than the mistake. Human error happens, but human fixes make up the difference. Don't take it out on the server's tip.

DON'T ASSUME WE ARE NOT PROFESSIONALS.

Never suggest that your service staff aspires to anything other than simply doing the best job they can. Gone are the days when every server was putting themselves through college or waiting for a big Hollywood break. "So, what do you do? I mean other than this?" No matter how you slice it, such a statement sounds condescending.

DON'T LEAVE YOUR MANNERS AT HOME.

You should never snap your fingers, impatiently clear your throat or perform some similar gesture to get the staff's attention. We all have names, and if you don't know it, a simple "Excuse me" goes a long way.

DON'T HIT ON THE SERVER.

I mean *ever*. It's just uncomfortable for everyone, including you, and really has all sorts of headache written all over it. Trust me, the server is being just as nice to you as they are to everyone else.

NEVER BERATE THE STAFF.

This is pretty much a good rule in any industry. Why is it okay for you to complain because we ran out of the dish you wanted or don't have the reservation time you requested? The place I've seen this happen most is at the airport. How is it okay to yell at the gate attendant, "You better get me on that flight"? The entire plane is delayed or overbooked, and the gate attendant clearly didn't make it happen (see number 2).

DON'T BE A NO-SHOW.

Restaurants are in the business of making money. I often hear, "I can't believe that restaurant closed. It was my favorite and always so hard to get into." Perhaps you couldn't get a reservation because it was always booked full, but now it's closed because of all the reservations that weren't kept. Making reservations at several restaurants for the same time and then deciding where to go at the last minute is the height of egotism. Yes, we keep a waitlist, but typically by the time your reservation time arrives (and you don't) those on the waitlist have already made other plans. If you can't make it, that's fine; we understand that stuff happens. But at least have the courtesy to call as soon as you know. Empty seats on busy Saturdays make for a short-lived business.

DON'T PULL THE YELP CARD.

If things go wrong, speak up about it right then and there. But do so in a polite and productive manner. Threatening a staff member or manager with a bad Yelp review is tantamount to saying, "I'm gonna tell my mommy on you." It's childish and unproductive. And what's worse is keeping your concerns to yourself while at the restaurant and then sharing them with the world later on the Internet. If you really want us to right a wrong, speak up! Any restaurant professional will go out of their way to assist you. If your first inclination is to complain to nameless, faceless people, you likely were never going to be pleased in the first place.

PART SIX

DAYS OF WINE

*Every once in a while,
that burger and fries screams
for a 1961 Cheval Blanc.*

No Merlot!

How an independent film turned our wine service upside down

AN ODD THING STARTED happening in late 2004 that made me wonder what was going on in the world of wine. It began suddenly, then quickly turned into an epidemic that lingered for months.

I would approach a table where guests were perusing the wine list, and ask, "May I help with your wine selection?" The typical response is appreciation, but during this strange time, it came with a twist.

"Absolutely. We are looking for a bottle to enjoy throughout our meal—soft enough for the early courses, but bold enough to stand up to the entrée." A reasonable request. But all reason flew out the window when they'd add, emphatically, *"Just no merlot!"*

That peculiar caveat soon became an asterisk to nearly every wine request. The problem for me was that most of my go-to wines at that time were from the west coast of Tuscany, in Bolgheri, and very often featured merlot as a primary component.

As weeks passed I experienced this boycott more frequently, and the guests became more adamant. Some even displayed a touch of anger if I tried to slip some merlot past them.

"Here is one of my favorites," I would say, presenting one of the finest labels in our cellar. "It's produced on an estate near the famed Sassicaia. It's called Le Macchiole, and their Bolgheri DOC is a blend of cab Franc, Syrah and merl—"

I couldn't even get the entire word out of my mouth before they would pounce: *"No merlot!"*

Out of nowhere, I, an experienced sommelier, was getting lambasted for suggesting one of the primary grape varietals in the world. It was the equivalent of a waiter being told, "Feed us anything you want; *just no pasta!"*

One evening I decided to get to the bottom of this. I was determined to offer a merlot-based wine to the first customer who asked my assistance, and prepared for the inevitable response.

"I have a great wine that I just fell in love with. It's California, lush, full-bodied, not at all harsh, with a fair amount of oak, and although unfiltered it has an elegance I think you will enjoy. It's called Newton Unfiltered Merlot."

"Merlot? *No merlot!* Do you have anything without merlot?"

"Of course I do, and I am happy to make other suggestions. But first, do you mind if I ask you a quick question?"

"Sure."

"Lately, every time I suggest a merlot-based wine, it is immediately rejected. As recently as a month ago these wines were the most popular on our list, and now all of the sudden, without so much as a taste, I'm told to find other wines with a strict no-merlot policy. Have you always said 'no' to merlot, or is this a recent change in your taste?"

The customer looked at me incredulously. "Haven't you seen the movie *Sideways?*"

My blank stare revealed that I hadn't. I was working a lot at the time, and sitting through a movie on my day off wasn't an option.

"Paul Giamatti is a wine connoisseur who takes his friend to Santa Barbara wine country for one last boys' weekend before the friend's wedding. They visit wineries and taste lots of varieties, but there is one rule: *No merlot!* It really highlighted to us that we should expand our horizons, too. So we stopped drinking merlot."

A movie. Really? Our merlot sales—not to mention merlot sales nationwide—were severely diminished thanks to a fictional character in a movie. Now that is some power of suggestion. I had to see this movie, and the next time I had a couple of hours, I did.

Giamatti was excellent in his role. But his down-and-out writer and self-made wine snob had an illogical distaste for merlot that ran like a ribbon through the film. His mantra—"Just no merlot!"— seemed to be no more than a social outcast's flippant reaction to the grape's popularity. If the masses liked it, it must not be good.

Meanwhile, throughout the film the character continually refers to his prized 1961 Cheval Blanc, which he is saving for the absolutely perfect moment—hopefully the sale of his next book. But when the book deal falls through, he finally realizes that the wine makes the occasion—not the other way around—and decides to drown his sorrows by drinking the rare vintage out of a paper cup along with a takeout burger and fries.

Of course, I have no problem at all with the character's choice of occasion to open the prized bottle. But what I do have a problem with is the fact that Cheval Blanc is made from—wait for it—merlot!

I'm sure that killing the merlot market wasn't the screenwriter's intent, but the effect that movie had on my business was chilling. Luckily, the trend ended after a while, and the wonderful grape finally reclaimed its rightful place. But the experience did illustrate just how easily swayed people can be, and it exposed the fact that self-professed wine aficionados can have some pretty shady sources for their education and opinions.

Even after realizing how and why merlot had come under fire, I vowed not to school any customer who was fixated on the "*No merlot!*" mantra. And I was determined not to let their innocent ignorance get my goat. Instead, I simply helped them navigate the rest of our wine list and gave selection advice only when solicited. My sole purpose, as always, is to ensure that they have a good time. As Giamatti's character illustrated, sometimes a burger and fries screams for a 1961 Cheval Blanc.

And who am I to stop you?

The Amateur Expert

"Since I know how much these bottles cost,
I simply cannot see myself paying list price"

THE SIDEWAYS PHASE passed and we were back to selling merlot by fall. Of course, that didn't mean that all self-proclaimed wine aficionados had turned in their badges.

The amateur wine expert—oxymoron intended—is a segment of our customer base that will never go away. We couldn't be happier about that. For no other reason, they sure keep things interesting. If every customer who visited our restaurants presented the same needs and quirks, what boring nights we'd have.

Within the fraternity of wannabe sommeliers, there is a wide range of opinion, attitude and communication style. But the one constant is the desire to let me know just how ridiculously high the pricing on restaurant wine is. When we opened Vetri, I didn't know to expect this chorus that regularly challenged our pricing. But it didn't take long before I would have to face the music.

I approached a table of four one evening, and a gentlemen had the wine list open to a specific page as he continued to engage with the rest of his party. He seemed to be painstakingly holding a finger on a particular spot, which indicated to me that he was ready to order.

I leaned in and quietly asked, "Pardon the interruption, but have you selected a wine?"

"Not just yet," replied the man with the list.

"My apologies, it looked like you were holding a place. Please let me know if you need assistance or if you do make a selection."

"Well, I was just showing my friend this particular bottle," he said, and lifted the list to show me the object of his attention. His finger was pointing to a price, so I scanned across the page to see he had selected a nice Amarone.

"Yes, I love that wine, especially now in the winter since it pairs so well with our richer dishes."

"Oh, yes, I'm familiar with it, too. I have it at home in my cellar."

"Then maybe we can find a similar bottle that you don't have, so you can try something new?"

"Sure, that'll be fine," he replied, although there was a clear change in his tone. I couldn't place my finger on what caused the change, but ignored it while I perused the list and made a new suggestion. The gentleman nodded with a slight smile, subtly noted that it cost less than the Amarone, and approved the selection.

The man seemed to enjoy himself throughout the evening, but I couldn't help noticing that our rapport had deteriorated, and I couldn't figure out why. I had been cordial yet friendly, had selected an appropriate wine and was certain that I had not been overly intrusive. The rest of the party also seemed to enjoy their meals, and they politely thanked us on the way out. It wasn't a disaster by any stretch, but I felt I'd lost a customer. Although I've had trouble making connections with guests on occasion, in this case I had made a connection and then lost it. I wanted to understand why, but figured I'd missed my opportunity.

To my delight, when I came in the next day there was a reservation request on the answering machine left by the gentleman from the night before. I assumed he must have really enjoyed his evening after all, and better yet, I would have a second chance to engage him. We don't often get second chances, so I wasn't going to squander it.

The reservation day arrived, and in walked the gentleman and his wife, along with a new couple. I greeted them at the door, escorted them to their table and delivered menus. As I reached across the table to hand a menu to the gentleman's wife, an unusual thing happened: the man retrieved a bottle from a bag that I had not noticed, and set it on the center of the table. I immediately realized it was the same Amarone that he had pointed to on our list the last time.

Puzzled, I asked, "Sir, what should I do with this bottle?"

"Well, open it. It's been standing upright in my cellar but I didn't have a chance to decant it, so we need it to breathe. Oh, by the way, I never called to ask, but what is your corkage fee?"

His words and tone were like a one-two combination to the gut. The word "corkage" alone would have stopped me in my tracks. I had never seriously considered offering corkage, for the obvious reasons that we spent a lot of money to acquire a license to serve alcohol and we sank even more resources into curating a top-flight cellar. And let's not forget that the wine he had asked me to open is one that I sell, for profit, to make a living.

I knew that calling out this customer was not an option, for several reasons. First, of all the possible responses that immediately crossed my mind, none of them would have been considered good customer service. Second, the fact that he had had the audacity to plan and execute such an action told me that he wouldn't understand—or care—if I tried to explain why I didn't want to open his bottle. And finally, I didn't want to embarrass him, no matter how much he was now going to embarrass me.

I took a deep breath and regained my composure.

"Sir, unfortunately we do not offer corkage as yet. It is something we have been discussing, but to this point, we have a cellar that does go pretty deep so I hope we can find something to your liking on our list."

"What do you mean, 'to my liking'? Obviously this bottle here is to my liking; it's on your list."

"Exactly, sir. It's on our list, so it is something that we sell. If we *were* to offer a corkage in the future, I think we would likely exclude wines that are on our list, or it wouldn't make sense to have the list."

"No, what doesn't make sense is that I paid $45 for this bottle, and I see it on your list for $110. Why would I pay you two and a half times what I paid for it?"

And now I finally knew what set him off during his first visit. He needed to let us know that he was a wine expert with a cellar and that he had uncovered our deep, dark secret: that we were in business to make a profit!

At that point, we had reached a crossroads. Whatever I said next would dictate not only how the rest of our evening would go, but could also affect our other guests' evening if I didn't choose the right words.

"Sir, we are in business not only to please our guests, but to make a living for ourselves and our staff. If you owned a cattle farm, would you bring your own steak to our restaurant and ask us to cook it for a nominal fee because you paid a fraction of what we paid for it? Of course you wouldn't. . . ."

Those are the words I wanted to say, but didn't.

Instead, I said, "Sir, I would love to open that bottle for you this evening, particularly since you said you did not realize we do not offer corkage. Because you are already here and have brought the bottle, let's do it. But for future visits, we would request that you order wine from our list. That is, of course, unless we do implement a corkage plan."

"Thank you so much. It's just that I put so much time and effort into my cellar too. Since I *know* how much these bottles cost, I simply cannot see myself paying list price. I know you need to make a living, but connoisseurs like myself would never go to a restaurant with a limited list like this unless we could bring our own. That's why the BYOB craze is so hot. No offense, but not everyone has a cellar like I do."

That is what he said, but not what he meant.

Instead, he meant to say, "I knew you would give me what I want. That's why I didn't call first. If I had called first, you would've said, 'No, we don't offer corkage,' and then I would have looked like a bad person when I brought the bottle anyway. This way, I have you by the short hairs because I noticed last time how eager you were to please your guests. I took advantage of that, brought my own wine, had a great meal, saved a few bucks and guess what? I'm not coming back anyway, so it really is no skin off my back."

After that experience, I developed a stronger backbone, became less apologetic for the fact that we actually make a profit and to this day we still don't offer corkage at Vetri.

And of course, I never saw that guy again.

The Price of Wine

It's a lot more than just math

I'M GOING TO LET YOU IN on a little secret: We mark up our food costs far more than we do our wine costs.

Restaurant wine pricing is a hotly discussed topic, whether the conversation is an anonymous one among strangers online or a spirited one among friends at a restaurant table. Most guests don't really think about the mark-up on our wines; they are out for a good time and typically choose their bottle based on any number of factors that do not include the restaurant's perceived profit. But for the vocal minority of guests who *do* question this one factor, it can be a topic of grave concern, as we've already seen. Any perception that a particular wine is "too" marked-up can compel an otherwise reasonable person to make a scene. I'm looking at you, Mr. Amarone!

The fact is, there is so much more than basic math that goes into wine pricing, and you need to see the whole picture to appreciate every aspect of our list, including the prices.

First, let's consider the mark-up on food. Our customers are happy to order whatever interests them on our menu without the slightest thought of mark-up. They may balk at the price of a more expensive dish, but rarely if ever do they consider margin when deciding what to eat. I suspect that the average customer's internal justification—if they had one at all—would go something like this: "Sure, I can go to the store and buy a steak and cook it just like the restaurant can, but even if they get a bulk discount they still have a chef and staff who invent new recipes, go out and acquire the steak, season it, expertly cook it to my liking and then serve it at just the right moment."

Most guests simply accept the fact that when they show up at a restaurant, the price they pay for the food will be significantly higher than what they pay for raw ingredients at the market. Not so with wine. At least not for the subset of customers who've never seen a wine list that didn't give them a conniption!

There has always been a perception that restaurants are out to get you when it comes to alcohol pricing in general, and wine pricing in particular. Surely you've heard someone say about a restaurant, "Oh, they make all their profits on alcohol." And while everyone seems to inherently know this, for some reason when they become the consumer all hell breaks loose. But I assure you, we do not make all our profits from wine. Not when you consider everything that goes into curating the list.

I have personally spent countless hours researching wine pricing, especially since we are based in a state (Pennsylvania) that controls all alcohol sales, sets pricing and adds their own severe mark-up before I place my order. I won't get too technical on the variation of laws from state to state, but suffice it to say that things are different in New York, California, Texas and elsewhere. In fact, if we were legally able to drive across the Delaware River into New Jersey to purchase our stock, it would surely affect our pricing. So geographical location is the first factor to consider, and there are many others.

The bottom line is, there's no one-size-fits-all pricing structure for wine. From restaurant to restaurant there are different views and systems employed. Some just make a specific dollar-value mark-up on every bottle—say $10 or $15 or $20—and call it a day. Whether the bottle costs them $20 and they charge $40, or it costs $100 and they charge $120, they make $20 per bottle and their work is done.

But others—including Vetri—use a more complex formula that considers a variety of factors. For example, my mark-up percent on a higher-priced bottle will always be much lower than that of a less-expensive one. If I tried to use a standard rate, say double the cost, then I'd have to charge $200 for a $100 bottle. I don't need to do that to the consumer, and besides, they would see right through it. However, if I pay $10 for a bottle, it's not unheard of for me to charge $20, which is the same mark-up. So right off the bat we have a sliding scale of the metrics.

But as I said earlier, there is more to wine pricing than just math. Consider the chef who can speak about the origin of a dish by pointing to his education, travels, inspirations, failures and successes. In essence, he is saying "I've learned my craft, traveled the world honing it, worked it and lived it for years, and now I'm going to open my heart for you when I put this food on your plate." Similarly, a sommelier can weave a tale that ends with a recommendation for a bottle that will elevate your dining experience to its utmost.

Just before we opened Vetri in 1998, I had to make a quick study of the wine landscape and travel to Italy in order to stock our cellar. I believed at the time that I did a good job of complementing what Marc was trying to accomplish with the food. But at the end of our first year, Marc and I went to Italy together for the first time and my life changed forever.

That first visit focused on the annual wine show in Verona called Vinitaly. This massive trade show features virtually every producer from every region of Italy over the course of a week. But it only takes a few hours to realize that there is much more in the bottle than juice. On day one we explored the Piedmont pavilion, tasting that region's wines including Barolo, Barbaresco, Barbera and Dolcetto. The information and emotion I was exposed to in those first few hours was eye-opening. But the best part was sitting down for a conversation with Atillio Pecchenino, one of the up-and-coming winemakers at the time. We tasted some of the Dolcetto he was making in Dogliani (a lesser-known area for Dolcetto than the more familiar Alba). He poured a beautiful glass of Siri Jermu, an unfiltered wine the likes of which I hadn't experienced. And I fell in love with a single-vineyard label called San Luigi. All the while he talked about everything that went into winemaking—what he learned from his ancestors, where he grew the grapes, what the terrain was like, how the soil composition affected the process, how different varieties interact. He described the wines he planned on making, and his excitement became mine.

Soon after tasting the San Luigi, his friend and colleague Elvio Cogno joined us. Like Atillio, Elvio was a young winemaker who had learned his craft from an earlier generation. He was excited about a Cogno Barolo he was making so we sat and drank a glass as he described its background. That afternoon more friends came and went, sharing stories and information, which I absorbed like a sponge. Each of them would say things like, "Hey Jeff, you've got to taste this wine; it's made just next to our vineyard, but it's a bit closer to the foothills of the valley and the sun doesn't shine there as much, so it's a little cooler climate." After six hours I stood up and was reminded how much wine I had drunk, but I was elated and thought that life couldn't get much better. I was wrong!

On day two, we hit the Lombardia pavilion featuring winemakers from the region where Marc had spent most of his time in Italy. On this day I would meet many of the local friends who had shaped Marc's experiences. I didn't think my time with Atillio and Elvio could be topped, but it was when I met the world-famous Maurizio Zanella. From the hilltop of his Ca' Del Bosco winery you can gaze upon the snow-capped peaks of the Alps to the north. This region is the home of Franciacorta, an area whose reputation for excellent sparkling wines rivals that of Champagne, thanks in large part to Maurizio himself. Of course I had had plenty of experiences with sparkling wines, but that day my appreciation for them grew exponentially as I drank, listened and learned. Conversely, Maurizio was excited to hear Marc describe how he had brought his Lombardian influences back to Philadelphia with great success. We met with many others throughout the day, from the established owners of Bella Vista to a young winemaker who was producing Franciacorta in his small winery, Monzio Compagnoni. As we sat and drank the upstart's Brut Saten, it occurred to me on the spot that bubbles needn't be reserved for special celebrations; they also work whenever friends get together.

Several years later, after Vetri had reached unforeseen heights, Marc and I took our second trip to Italy, this time adding the destination of Friuli in the far northeast corner. By then I had been to Italy alone many times, my passion for wine had grown exponentially and my understanding of it continued to unfold like the layers of an onion. I had spent so much time with Marc's Italian friends and family that I was starting to feel at home with them myself. It was on this trip that we enjoyed an unforgettable experience with Mario Batali and his business partner Joe Bastianich, friends from back in the States. Joe, a wine guru in his own right, had recently opened the Bastianich Vineyard in Friuli, not too far from where his family had lived. The drive to Friuli was breathtaking, and it was remarkable to see the signs start to include German and English words beside Italian, letting you know that this Italian winemaking region is clearly different from the others. At the time I had grown enamored of the white Ribolla Gialla grape, which was grown both in Friuli and across the border in Slovenia. And while I had expected to taste some beautiful white wines that are the hallmark of that area's cooler climate, I was pleasantly surprised by the quality of Joe's Refosco, which originates from the dark-skinned grape also found in the region.

Upon arrival Joe loaded us into his little Yugo sedan and drove us around his growing vineyard, pointing out something different every minute. "That's where we're going to put the guest house. And see that empty building over there? That's where the vats will go.

Over there is where we are going to age the wine, and the grapes you see up on that hill are Tocai, which is now called Friulano. And look over that way, across the hills—that's Slovenia. It's the home of Movia, one of my favorite wineries, and also of Ales Kristancic, one of the greatest winemakers I have ever met, not to mention one of the craziest people I know!"

Toward day's end we pulled up near the main building, where a pig turned on a spit over an open fire. Friends milled about, and others continued to arrive as the hour passed. Our pal Leonardo LoCascio, who owns Winebow Importers, was there. So were a few fellow restaurateurs, a prominent wine writer and about forty others we met for the first time. We were escorted into a giant dining room, and before long Joe had butchered the pig, made risotto, opened numerous bottles of wine and kicked off the feast. We ate and drank like kings all night, sharing stories and news about the topic we all loved best. At evening's end we were treated to an operatic solo performed by Joe, who has an amazing voice. It was one of the finest nights of my life.

One result of that night was my discovery of, and subsequent love affair with, Joe's Tocai Plus, made from the Friulano grape with a little bit of sugar and a nice sweet finish. For weeks afterwards all I would talk about with guests was this amazing trip to Joe's vineyard. I probably sold more Tocai Plus that year than I've ever sold. I ended up drinking quite a bit myself as guests noticed my unbridled passion and offered me a glass and a seat. It was clear that my own love for this wine—culled from knowledge I had gained in Italy—translated to our guests.

So what goes into the pricing of a bottle of wine? It would take forever to try to determine exactly where on the sliding scale any particular bottle's price falls. Suffice it to say that what goes into it may be a journey to Verona, a drive through the hillside vineyards, a lineage of people crafting their trade and many hours of intense conversation, questions and revelations. What goes into it is a lot more than a dollar value on the price tag.

So if you want more value out from your bottle of wine, ask

your sommelier to tell you a little something about it. You may just find yourself traveling to a hillside village in Italy.

The Price of Corkage

Setting standards for the pop-your-own-cork crowd

SINCE MY run-in with the Amateur Expert and his bootlegged bottle of Amarone, the wine list at Vetri has grown to the point that I can say with confidence that we will never offer corkage on a regular basis at Vetri, and there is a very good reason why. But that's not to say we won't open a bottle that a regular guest brings on occasion, or that we're against the notion in general. In fact, all of our other restaurants do allow guests to bring a bottle and have us hold, chill, open and serve it for a modest fee.

The first question anyone asks when inquiring if corkage is available at a restaurant is, "How much?" And just like pricing a bottle of wine, there are specific factors that have to be considered.

Amis, our neighborhood trattoria, includes a more select wine list than Vetri, although it does offer choices to complement everything on the menu. We've got all the main grapes and regions of Italy covered, with various options for each. But we realize that some guests want to bring their own special bottle, and for them there's a standard corkage fee of $25. To anyone who does go this route, I encourage you to ask the sommelier for their thoughts on your bottle. It is our pleasure to talk wine at any time, and it's always good to hear guests' take on the bottle they brought. You may even learn something new.

Our corkage fee at Pizzeria Vetri, on the other hand, is even lower at $15 a table, partly because of the more casual atmosphere and partly because the wine list is even more restricted due to our focus on offering an extraordinary beer selection. Yet everything else about our wine service remains intact—we wouldn't have it any other way.

I've been to very nice restaurants that charge a hundred bucks a pop for corkage, and to me, that seems more like a penalty than a courtesy. That would be an unthinkable proposition in our world. If you really don't want people to bring their own, why not just charge a thousand?

Our stance at Vetri is really not about money at all. Sure, we could charge an obscene fee to pop your cork, and obviously we do make a profit when we sell you our bottles. But anyone who thinks that economics is the primary reason for keeping our wine service in house is missing the point. We want you to have the full Vetri experience when you dine with us, and a major part of that experience is our wine service.

Our cellar represents every important vineyard, every grape, and every price point you may desire. Your server or sommelier will ask about your likes and dislikes, menu choices for the evening, and past wine experiences to start the process, and the conversation only gets better from there. For many, wine selection is one of the most enjoyable parts of the evening—and that's before you even take a sip!

But we are flexible, especially the more we get to know you. One of our frequent regulars has been bringing his own bottles of wine to Vetri since we opened over sixteen years ago, and he continues to do so. The catch is, he only brings a bottle on his birthday, and he always tries to impress or surprise me with his finds. And more often than not, he succeeds. The rest of the year—and he dines with us frequently—he orders from our list and asks me to choose his wine every visit.

We have another couple who show up at times with two identical bottles in tow—one to drink with their meal, and one as a gift for us. Like the birthday boy, they make it a game to try to wow me with their finds. And as aficionados with impressive connections in the wine industry, they always deliver. They've been doing this for years, and it's always brought great enjoyment to all three of us. About a year ago, they called one day before making a reservation to make sure I'd be there on the night of their choice.

"We've got something really special this time. You're going to love it."

"I'm intrigued! But I have to ask a favor," I replied. "Please don't bring the wine bottles into the restaurant anymore," I said. "Don't get me wrong—you can still bring the wine! You know that we always love having you, and we appreciate your gifts. It's just a matter of appearance. As you know, we don't offer corkage at Vetri, so I think it's better if you drop off the bottles in the kitchen first, then walk around to the dining room entrance. If others see you carrying in your own bottles, they may get the wrong idea—I don't want to start a trend! Just give me a call when you're nearby and we'll be ready for you. I hope you understand."

To this day, they continue to bring two bottles on the occasional visit, always setting up the drop-off ahead of time. And not only do they not mind the new procedure, they say they get a kick out of the covert aspect of it all.

Of course, back-door drop-off BYOB is not something that we plan to institute for other guests. But even if we did, I suspect that not many would take advantage of the possibility—not when they know what they get when they embrace the full Vetri experience.

PART SEVEN

PUTTING SYSTEMS IN PLACE

*"Yeah, we ran a little late. Sorry.
And oh yeah, we are now
six and not four."*

Greeting and Seating

You don't have to see how the sausage is made to enjoy it

Friends of ours own the fantastic restaurant Arrows in Ogunquit, Maine, and one night some years ago I made a reservation to dine there with my wife. I could have sworn that the reservation was for 6:45 p.m.; that's the time I had written down in my planner. So we showed up promptly with great anticipation.

Well, apparently there is no such thing as a 6:45 reservation at Arrows. We were actually slated for six o'clock and were forty-five minutes late on a busy Saturday night. I was mortified; I knew exactly how bad a mistake I had made. My face turned beet red and I apologized profusely.

"Is there anything we can do? We'll eat fast. We won't order dessert. We'll eat in the car!"

The host just looked me in the eye, smiled and said, "It's not your problem. It's our problem."

We ended up having a great meal that night after just a slight delay, as they were quick to make arrangements to seat us and serve us, with no strings attached. Clearly it was my fault, but Arrows took the blame and created a solution.

I'll never forget the smoothness and calmness with which they made things right that night, with zero attitude or admonishment. While it's always been our policy in the Vetri Family to fix such mistakes with grace, it was a learning experience to see it from a guest's point of view. Please, don't take this the wrong way and decide it's okay to show up anytime, knowing a solution will always be found! Because when a guest misses their reservation time by more than fifteen minutes, without calling to let us know, it really does screw things up. Actually, it's one of the rudest things a guest can do, second only to those who make a reservation, never show up and never bother to call.

They say you don't have to see how the sausage is made to enjoy it. Some go so far as to say that if you do see how the sausage is made, you may no longer enjoy it. Well, the simple step of arriving at a restaurant is actually sausage-making at its finest. Just know that all things happen by design, and that it all starts when you walk through our door.

Whatever table-management system a restaurant employs—even if they still use paper and pencil—it is only as good as the person using it. Most of the time, that is the host, who is also the first person our guests see upon arrival. Talk about pressure! The host staff is responsible for knowing which tables are almost finished, how many we are expecting to see in the next half hour, which tables are in danger of overstaying their welcome and how much space we have for walk-ins. Not to mention about a dozen other responsibilities. And all this must be done with a sincere smile.

Actually, so much happens in the first thirty seconds of your arrival that we have a separate manual specifically for the host staff. It explains how to operate the computer system to mark a guest as arrived, seated, apps, entrées, dessert and paid. Yes, the host is tracking you throughout the evening, and that information is also sent to the servers, manager, captain and maître d'. The host uses this system to determine the ideal table to seat each guest so that seatings flow as efficiently as possible. She must know at all times how many tables are in each server's section and where each of those parties are in their meal so the servers never get overwhelmed, as well as how many tables that are currently deuces might need to pair with adjacent tables to create four tops and six tops at the next turn. It's a lot to keep under control in a fluid situation where timing is everything and guests' expectations are all heightened. But wait, there's more!

The manual also factors in countless what ifs. What if a guest doesn't like their table? What if a guest shows up late or with more people than originally booked? What if a guest shows up on the wrong day or even at the wrong restaurant? What if there's a traffic jam, the babysitter doesn't show on time, the guest gets a flat tire or six straight tables all decide they're having such a good time that they stay thirty minutes longer than slated? It all happens all the time, and it's all in the manual. We try to imagine and document everything that could go wrong, so that when situations arise, they don't go wrong—and if they do, at least we'll be prepared to make them right. But just when you think you've seen and heard it all, people come up with new and creative situations for the host to handle. Consider this scenario, which often takes place during the busiest time of year.

Dateline: Saturday night, autumn, 7:30 p.m.

"Hi, we're the Johnson party. We have a reservation."

Usually on arrival the party will state their name, number of people *and* reservation time. When they omit the number and/or the time, it's a dead giveaway—usually done intentionally because they've held to neither and are hoping we have somehow forgotten the details.

"Oh yes. Welcome. I have you down for a party of four. If you could just give me a moment, I will see which tables may be available. We had you listed for a 6:30 arrival."

"Yeah, we ran a little late. Sorry. And oh yeah, we are now six and not four. I'm sure that won't be a problem. In fact, I see an empty table right over there. We can squeeze in if we need to. Sound good?"

That's not how it works. That's not how any of this works!

From the guest's single statement, we understand not only their expectations, but how little wiggle room they're giving us to fix a problem they've created. They indicated they have no understanding of how reservations work; if they did, they wouldn't have arrived so late without so much as a call, and they certainly wouldn't have added to their party without checking availability.

You may sense some attitude here, but I'm just telling it like it is. The more important reality is that we have a strong desire and commitment to please every guest to the extent we can, without compromising our service standards. But really, how does one explain that the empty table over there is actually reserved for a soon-to-arrive four top to a party who apparently has no clue? Delicately!

"Sir, that table is for a reservation that is arriving now."

"But we had a reservation an hour ago."

I could have told you that was going to be his reply! To which the logical response would be: "Yes, and had you arrived an hour ago, you would now be thirty minutes from departure and we wouldn't be having this conversation."

Of course, that's not what we say. Instead, we say, "Of course, and I am going to find you the best table that would accommodate both you and the soon-to-arrive 7:30 reservations."

It's funny how quickly a guest can assimilate all the training and knowledge that it takes to be a successful restaurant host. Because when the empty table reserved for the 7:30 four top is denied them, they quickly scan the room and move on to Plan B or C or D.

"Excuse me, hostess? I notice that the people over there are finishing their dessert. Should only be a matter of minutes before we can replace them!" Or, "Hey look, that table is getting up. That should work for us, right?" Or, "I just saw that guy pull out his credit card! They must be paying. Let me go get the rest of my party."

In the worst-case scenario, they will start hovering over a table that seems to be nearing conclusion of their heretofore enjoyable meal. No one can hide the hover; it's always as noticeable as a canker sore to the victims. It is in these moments that the job of host expands to include the responsibility of police officer. Hopefully, we are able to encourage the late and extra-large party to visit the bar while we sort out the configuration. Don't forget, it's the busiest time of the year, so while this whole farce is unfolding many other guests are arriving on time and expecting to be seated. And for our late friends, there's nothing worse than to witness other guests who arrived after you being seated in what seems to be your place.

Just trust our plan. Acknowledge your responsibility in the matter, relax and put yourself in our hands. We know who is slated to go where, when they should go there and who is scheduled to be finished when. We also have all the variables covered and can quickly work through it. Our host staff, like hawks seeking prey, have developed a keen thirty-thousand-foot aerial view of the room and see it as one giant slow-moving picture rather than the fast-as-hell slam dance that it appears to be in real time on the ground.

And there's the rub. Individuals, rightfully so, only concern themselves with their own situation. So an empty table shouldn't be empty if they need it, and if they have a reservation and it's past that time, nobody should be seated until they have been, regardless of any other factors including those of their own making. At times, the two views do collide and, under the wrong circumstances, can create a disastrous situation with angry guests, flustered staff and potentially lost business. But we spend a lot of time with the host staff on what seems like minutiae so that we don't have one hot minute when the doors open. If only guests would realize that the two minutes they spend at the host stand took us hours to orchestrate, just so that we start off their night on the right foot.

So... now that you know what happens when you cross our threshold, there's only one thing left to say.

Welcome! Let's get this party started—even if you're late!

The Bar

It's not just about alcohol sales

IF I'M LOOKING at our restaurant as an extension of my house, then the bar is definitely the den, or even better, the finished basement. It is the area that most exudes relaxation. No matter what kind of restaurant you choose to dine in, if they have a bar it should be an area where you hear occasional laughter and where guests feel comfortable whether sitting on a stool or standing. There's an air of familiarity with the bar staff that may not exist at the same level with everyone else. The music in that area is often a bit louder, and if the bar has TVs, you'll see heads tilted catching the score of the game even if they aren't fans—it's all part of the camaraderie.

As with everything else we do, that casual and enticing air is no accident. With the exception of the kitchen, no area occupies more of our preopening planning sessions than the bar. Folks outside the industry would probably say, "Of course, that's where you make your money—alcohol sales are marked up so high that if we just came and drank you'd be happy." There may be a bit of truth to that, but the generalization oversimplifies and understates the bar's real importance. Alcohol sales, while providing great margins, only make up about 30 percent of our revenue company-wide. And besides, you probably wouldn't come to the bar if you didn't like our food as well.

In most restaurants the bar is an amenity, albeit a profit-driven one, but it should always exist first to enhance guests' enjoyment. Without taking care of that step, there'd be no profit. I'm not sure of the exact numbers, but whether guests choose to have a drink at the bar before they're seated or agree to wait for their table there on a busy night, most people will find themselves at the bar at one time or another. That's why it always floors me when I go to a restaurant where the bar is clearly an afterthought.

Let's say you arrive early for your reservation and your table isn't ready. The host invites you to sit at the bar in the meantime. You walk toward the crowded bar, then realize you'll never get a seat, plus the bartender is ignoring you and chances are slim he'll get to your order. By the time the host comes to seat you, you are so frustrated that our service staff has their work cut out for them.

Now imagine the same scenario, except the bartender immediately makes eye contact. Within moments, he sees a barstool ready to be vacated and motions to you to take it. He asks if you're there for dinner or just a drink. When you answer dinner, he takes your order then quickly returns with cocktails, a little snack and a menu.

"I know you're sitting at a table, but I thought you might want to check out the menu to get excited for your meal," he says. You take the menu and ask him, "What are your favorite dishes?" Now dialogue begins. Maybe the bartender shares a few recommendations as he continues polishing glasses or restocking bottles. Or maybe he asks a question of his own. "Are you in the mood for pasta tonight? All of ours are homemade and very special. But so is the steak; it's from Creekstone Farms—premium Black Angus beef. "

In this scenario, by the time you're seated at your table, you are ready to savor an exceptional meal. You may even return to the bar for an after-dinner drink and to see who won the game.

A successful bar runs on a great staff, but the physical space needs to be inviting, too. A lavish display of bottles is both handsome and practical, enticing guests while revealing what's available. It's a chance to show off our aesthetic sensibilities too. Shiny beer taps with interesting logos pack the same punch.

We also design the surface of our bars to comfortably fit entrée plates for those who choose to dine there. It's frustrating when I have dinner at a bar someplace and the real estate is so small that I purposely avoid ordering the kind of hearty, expansive dishes I usually want. That's why we spend so much time with our designers having staff playact bartender-guest interactions and making sure there's sufficient space on both sides to ensure the guest's comfort.

When the bar is thoughtfully planned and properly stocked, it will always be well worth our guests' time. And it will be much more than simply thirty percent of our revenue. In fact, it will be the start of our relationship with you.

Taking Orders

How does she remember what everyone
ordered without writing it down?

WHAT'S SO HARD about taking orders?

Guests look at the menu, tell you what they want and you bring it to them. Seems pretty simple, right? I suppose it is, if that's all a diner wants out of the experience, or if that's all the staff wants to give them. With the bar set so low, yeah—anyone can do it.

But not in my world. The fact is, taking and delivering orders is the most critical responsibility of any front-of-house professional, and it entails remarkable mental and physical agility.

It is the server's job to:

1. Greet you immediately when you're seated
2. Answer all questions about beverage service
3. Take and remember drink orders
4. Accurately submit the drink orders to the service bar
5. Deliver each drink to the correct guest
6. Accurately describe daily specials and changes to the menu

7. Answer all questions about dishes on the menu
8. Take and remember your food orders
9. Accurately submit food orders to the kitchen
10. Deliver each plate to the correct guest
11. Clear and reset the table between courses
12. Answer questions about desserts
13. Take and remember your dessert orders
14. Accurately submit dessert orders to the kitchen
15. Deliver each dessert to the correct guest
16. Clear and reset the table after dessert
17. Take, make and deliver coffee orders to the correct guests
18. Clear coffee service and drop the check
19. Process payment

All of the above typically must happen within seventy-five minutes. Meanwhile, each server is simultaneously doing the same for three, four or five other tables. And that's just the nuts and bolts of the process on paper, assuming all goes as planned—which it never does. Those markers don't include running for more water, silverware and drinks; cleaning up spills; bringing unsatisfied diners' plates back to the kitchen to be cooked further or replaced; controlling pauses in service when guests visit the restroom or step outside to make a phone call and numerous other distractions. Whether or not it all works out smoothly, each step must be approached with a smile.

In addition to friendly but not obsequious service, many guests want actual guidance. This can take quite a few minutes to provide, and many hours to plan for. Some ask questions about ingredients, cooking methods, flavor profiles and whether the beef is grass-fed. Other guests have no idea what to order and are just hungry for a good suggestion. Either way, servers must know the menu inside-out.

Every server we employ, at all our restaurants, is empowered to answer any question about the menu, thanks to our "rigorous" training methods—i.e., we feed them. There's a lot to learn. One full day of every new training session is spent in the kitchen tasting everything on the menu. Staff members also spend part of the day watching dishes being prepared so they understand methods and cooking techniques. Training like this has its costs, but the returns are invaluable. Ask a Vetri Family server about any menu item and you'll never hear a toothless reply like, "Oh, that's a great dish," which most guests can tell is a generic non-answer.

We hired a server recently who came from a highly regarded restaurant in Center City where he'd worked since its opening. During training with us, on the day we brought him into the kitchen to taste the menu and watch food prep, he was flabbergasted. He compared our menu training to his last job and said there was no comparison. Literally.

Some restaurants believe that every nickel spent on food needs to bring back at least a dime. It's just about profit at all costs. So preparing food for servers to taste must seem ludicrous to them. The opposite is true in our estimation. You never know what a guest will ask, but you always have to be prepared to answer it.

It's not just new servers who get to taste. Each season when we change the menu, every server has the opportunity to eat and learn the entire new lineup of dishes. Best investment we could ever make. When a guest asks about our famous casoncelli pasta, they get a quick but detailed response. It not only gives them confidence to know what they want to order but also gives them a lot more information about the dish, which enhances their enjoyment.

Ironically, it's the generic questions that are literally impossible to provide answers to.

"Oh, I don't know what to order. What do you suggest?"

Servers hear that question a lot. To me, it's a trick question. The only acceptable answer is another question, if not a series of them. Whenever I hear a server reply with a specific suggestion from the menu, I cringe. How in the world could they know that would be a satisfactory choice for that guest? The only message such an answer sends is, "You are just an order, not a person."

Instead, a server needs to tease out the guest's desires: "Have you eaten here before? What are you in the mood for—something light, adventurous, classic? What wine are you thinking about? What did you have for lunch? How hungry are you? Do you want to each get something different and share? Do you have food allergies? Are there any ingredients to avoid? Do you have theater tickets or a game afterwards?" Servers don't have to ask a million questions every time; I tell them to just start asking until they see a spark in the guest's eye.

One common accusation about servers making suggestions is that we use them to push certain dishes, whether to move ingredients we have in excess or to sell high-profit items. If such factors make sense in the context of the order, of course we'll suggest them. But there are plenty of times when we make suggestions that actually get guests to order less.

Huh?

We serve pizza at a couple of our restaurants, and it's often shared among a table. When all four guests also order an individual appetizer and entrée, they're likely be full by the time the dessert course arrives. Depending on the group and the orders, the server may actually say something like, "You know, since you're ordering a large pizza for the table, I might suggest sharing the appetizer courses, too, and making it only two of those. Then order some entrées individually. I would hate for you to get so uncomfortably full that dessert or cheese isn't an option."

Such a suggestion has several effects. It lets the guests know you are concerned with their well-being. It creates trust, which in turn creates repeat customers. And it will likely get them to order four desserts and after-dinner drinks, giving them a well-rounded experience. You've also upsold without hammering them. And if they still don't order dessert, that's fine too; they'll be back!

People appreciate such thoroughness. The thing is, we also have to be efficient. While it would be great to stand around and discuss the finer points of grilling vs. broiling, side salad vs. fries, and double bock versus pilsner, remember, we've got seventy-five minutes to turn the table. That's why the best servers have honed their order-taking skills to maximize both efficiency and accuracy.

It is uncanny how a server can stand in front of a ten top, without the safety net of pen and paper, and remember every item ordered by each guest including salads, antipasti, appetizers, sides, and entrées, plus swaps, allergy warnings, cooking preferences, omissions and more. Some use mnemonic devices, often of their own creation, and others tune out the guest's extraneous thoughts, debates and stammering to just focus on what is actually being ordered. And when each person has finished, the server can quickly get to the POS system and key in all the info, including which guest gets which plate, with pinpoint accuracy. Some servers do need to rely on a paper trail, but typically they use a self-made shorthand so that they can continue to engage guests with eye contact throughout the process while ensuring an accurate order. That is an absolute must.

And then there is the delivery, which should never, ever go like this:

A server approaches a table of two holding two different entrées in his hands. He stops, stands there for a moment, then says to no one in particular, "Who got the pasta?"

There's no excuse for that to ever happen. Every restaurant employs some sort of system that assigns a number or letter to each seat at each table, and the orders include that information. So whether the server who took the order delivers the dishes, or they're brought out by a food runner, running a "dinner auction" just shows that nobody really knows what they're doing and creates an embarrassing moment for everyone. It's not so simple after all.

Checking In

We're just bit players in the evening's performance.
The guest is the star.

WHEN ALBERT EINSTEIN conceived the theory of relativity, I wonder if it occurred to him in a restaurant while waiting for his water glass to be refilled. After all, each minute that passes while your water glass is empty seems like an eternity, right?

In the restaurant business, as a rule, for every minute that passes the guest perceives it as five minutes. If you take three minutes to fix a problem, they think it took closer to fifteen. Who wants their guests to sit in disappointment for fifteen minutes? It's a crazy concept, but we have to treat this warped perception of time as reality. So when a guest says they've been waiting for fifteen minutes, it serves no purpose to reply, "Well, it's actually been *three* minutes, but okay…" The correct response is to acknowledge the concern and instantly resolve it—without the slightest hint that they may need a new watch battery.

One of our key training exercises gets right to the heart of the theory that time is relative. With the staff gathered in the dining room, I ask them to close their eyes and then raise their hand after five minutes have passed. After thirty years in this business, it no longer surprises me to see most hands go up within a minute or two. It also never surprises me to see the surprised looks on the faces of the time-challenged servers.

We teach this valuable lesson in the middle of systems training to highlight the importance of honing your internal clock while also calibrating it to jibe with the guests' perception of time. It's one thing to know the p's and q's of each system and to perfect them in a vacuum, but it's another thing to expertly apply them in the heat of the moment, all at the same time, in a loud room, among a number of people who expect to be served with precision and efficiency within a time frame that works for them. Not to mention with a smile.

Once you are seated, the server's goal is to minimize the amount of time spent away from your table so you will not be in need of anything for long. Not only do servers have to perform the balancing act of ensuring all of your needs are met, but they are performing the same act at the same time for four or five other tables. Great servers have honed their internal clocks to such a fine point that they can turn this cacophony into fluidity. They are acutely aware that when they serve drinks to Table One, the clock starts ticking and they've only got so many minutes until they should return. Meanwhile, thirty seconds have passed since they served the soup course to Table Two; a minute and a half has passed since they took food orders at Table Three; it's coming up on three minutes since they've checked on Table Four; and the food orders placed for Five seven minutes ago will be up in the kitchen for pickup in a minute or two.

Time is a major expectation in any walk of life, but possibly more so in the restaurant business since we're dealing with food temperatures and the fact that no one will begin eating until each person at the table has been served. Likewise, there is an expectation of the amount of time that should elapse between courses. Have I been waiting ten minutes for a pasta I know takes four minutes to make? Conversely, did I wait just four minutes for a pasta that should have taken ten, and does this mean they are trying to rush me, or worse, was the food precooked? All of these things come into play in a guest's mind; it's our job to squelch such doubts before they come on.

You can imagine how many balls are in the air throughout the evening's elaborate juggling act. Adding one more ball to the mix is the fact that we need to make a living, and so, besides serving each guest within the time frame their needs dictate, we also have the responsibility of turning tables within the time frame that we established when we set the night's reservations. If we know there should be roughly ten minutes between courses, the server needs to discern when a table is eating a little slower or a little faster, and take action by shaving off or adding on a minute here or there. But we also need to remember that two minutes can seem interminably long or curiously short, depending on the guest. We can clear, reset and re-serve two tables within the exact same time frame, and yet hear two different reactions: "They just cleared our plates and already they are dropping the next course," or, "We finished the last course twenty minutes ago; where's our next plate?" And although Einstein may agree with both parties, in reality we know that to clear a table, reset the silverware, get the glassware ready and refill all glasses takes just about four minutes on anyone's clock.

Exactly how do servers learn the mental gymnastics required to twist time every which way in order to make it all come out at the same place in the end? Fortunately, at Vetri, most of the servers we hire already have service experience, whether they worked at a diner, a mid-casual chain or even in fine dining. Once they go through orientation and initial training, their basic skills are refined to work within our systems. But it doesn't stop there. We train staff continuously, regardless of the level they've attained.

One of the most effective training exercises we use is role-play. We'll have a few staff members sit at tables and direct them to act like specific types of guests—a family gathering, a corporate powwow, a romantic dinner for two. Meanwhile, a couple of other servers will wait on them in a real-time scenario. The "guests" will pull no punches in demanding this and that, while the servers will try their best to create lifelong regulars. Not only do the servers get to work on a variety of skills—including balancing time expectations—but the "guests" get to experience the systems and timing from the real guests' point of view; that alone is a valuable lesson.

For more personal training, I'll have a server walk beside me and observe every table as we traverse the dining room, and when we get to the kitchen, I'll start grilling them.

"How many people still had food on their plate at Table Six? What course are they on at Seven? How many more minutes until the guests at Eight will be ready for the check?"

After a couple of decades in this business, I can briskly walk through a dining room and answer all those questions and more, about every table, at any time of the evening. And I expect all servers to develop that skill. In fact, one point that we constantly drive home in training is that every server should look at every table—not just their assigned tables—all night long. When this broad scope becomes a server's natural point of view, they are best prepared to step up and help each other whenever one needs a quick hand to get back on track.

I often hear colleagues say they get excited every single night when "the curtain goes up and the show starts." I understand what's meant by this common expression—like a theater, the room is quiet before the show begins and within an hour it's bustling with crazy energy. But I have mixed feelings about the line. On one hand, I don't believe that we're putting on a show, so to speak, although I do acknowledge the performance aspect of much of what we do. Instead, I compare what we do more to an orchestra, with movements perfectly directed by our maître d' or chef and carried out by individual servers who all come together to create a cohesive melody.

Even if we are considered performers, we are simply bit players. The guest is the star and needs to shine. As long as we understand our role and hit our marks, we will make beautiful music together.

Complaints and Comps

"You call this medium rare?"

NOT FOR NOTHING, but there's really nothing worse than doing nothing.

Any time a guest expresses dissatisfaction—whether they come out and say it or let their body language do the talking—it's a call to action. If they didn't get the table they'd requested, were perturbed by the loud group next to them or were not satisfied with their salad, the first thing we have to do is to do something.

It always starts with communication, and sometimes it ends with a complimentary dish or even full meal. But like everything else in this business, each case is a unique circumstance and should be treated with the proper response.

The irony is that every problem is actually an opportunity to turn around a frustrated guest. Believe it or not, it can be easier to satisfy a frustrated guest than it is to impress someone who comes in with unrealistic expectations. Ninety-nine times out of a hundred, the frustrated guest will react to our solution with a positive comment. Those are the moments you live for.

But before we get to the happy ending, we have to handle the situation in real time. Which brings me to the question: Exactly what is the guest's expectation for the restaurant to fix a problem? Typically, patrons do not come right out and ask for specific compensation, so it's up to us to assess the issue and match it with the solution that works for everyone. And we always make sure the balance leans in the customer's favor.

In recent years, many of the bigger restaurant chains have created an expectation that any complaint should score you a complimentary meal. The problem with this blanket fix is that it doesn't give the restaurant the opportunity to address the underlying problem for future guests. When I have a bad service experience as a consumer, I always take the opportunity to contact management and express my concerns, but with the caveat that I don't expect anything in return—my only motivation is to help them improve. I've actually turned down free stuff because I am sincere about this. But some people believe that any significant complaint should result in a free ride, and not just for a dish they didn't like—no, they want the restaurant to cover the entire bill. Before we go there, many things need to be considered.

Sometimes, a simple apology is all that's needed. Consider the common dilemma of a table not being ready immediately upon a guest's arrival. Often guests will grab a drink at the bar while they wait. But if you kid yourself into thinking they're happy being left alone to do so, you'd be wrong. Instead, keeping lines of communication open during their wait significantly mitigates their anxiety. The host or manager will approach several times with updates: "Excuse me, sir, the table just finished their last course; can I get you anything while you wait?" A couple minutes later: "Ma'am, your table is just about ready. We've dropped the check so it won't be long now." Three minutes later: "We've cleared the table and it's being set up for you now. We'll have you seated in a moment." This constant attention lets guests know things are moving forward, and more importantly, that they have not been forgotten.

Once the meal gets underway, there's a chance someone will be less than thrilled with a particular dish. Probably the most common issue is the guest's perception that a dish is undercooked or over-cooked. And if a dish arrives at the table in any manner other than what the guest wanted, regardless of whether or not it was in fact cooked to perfection, they still have every right to say, "I'd like this cooked differently." And we have every intention to do so, no questions asked.

Even if I had stood at the table while taking the order and said, "You realize that 'medium rare' means it is going to be slightly pink in the center," and it comes out slightly pink in the center, and the guest then says they do not want it that way, I'm still going to redo it. I'm not going to say, "Well I did, in fact, warn you ahead of time that it would be pink in the center…" That may be technically right, but in the sense of hospitality, it would be wrong.

Speaking of pink in the center, we serve a chicken dish at Osteria that is brined for twenty-four hours and then cooked in a wood-burning oven that exceeds 700 degrees. Because of the brining process and the high-temp searing, it's served with a pink tinge in the center despite the fact that it is fully cooked. Many people believe that an undercooked chicken will make them sick.

So one night we have a four top that seems to be really enjoying their meal. They cleaned up their vegetable antipasto and a couple of pizzas. For entrées, three ordered pasta and the fourth ordered the brined chicken. Moments after we dropped the plates, the chicken guy called over his server.

"My chicken's not fully cooked; I'm going to get sick," he said with a grimace.

"I'm so sorry sir, let me bring it back to the kitchen. I will cook it some more."

Now, you might have expected a different reply, possibly an explanation that this particular chicken dish always has a pink tint. But the server noted the guest's complete dismay and quickly determined that he could have explained until he was blue in the face, but that would not remove the pink tinge and this customer clearly wouldn't have it. So why argue?

If the guest was more inquisitive, an explanation may have sufficed, and a new fan of the dish may have been gained. But as it turned out, "Of course sir, let me cook it some more" is all that needed to be said.

"I don't want it cooked any more!" the guest said emphatically. "My taste for chicken has just disappeared because this looks disgusting and can't be fixed."

"Okay sir. I'm very, very sorry about that. Let me bring you a pasta dish, or something else, so I can make it up to you."

His friends, who had already started their pasta dishes—a chicken liver rigatoni and ravioli stuffed with porcini mushrooms—raved about their food, trying to put him at ease with the switch.

Most times the server's offer would be happily accepted, and both dishes—the chicken and the pasta replacement—would automatically be removed from the bill. The server need not even mention those adjustments; the guests will see it when they receive the check, and be satisfied with the result. Usually.

"I don't want pasta. I *wanted* chicken. But the chicken is bad and you've now ruined my meal."

"Well, I am so sorry you feel that way, sir. I'd really love to figure out a way to make it up to you."

"No, that's okay," he said and continued to pout.

Finally, the gentleman agreed to accept a pasta dish, and he seemed to do quite well with it, cleaning his plate. Even though his obvious satisfaction with the pasta should have meant the case was closed, we decided that we needed to take an extra step to completely win back this customer. So after their main course was cleared, we brought out our fantastic dessert board—a long wooden tray on which we plate almost every single one of our desserts. And on top of that, we sent out some gelato. If killing him with sweetness didn't do it, nothing would.

They ate every last crumb. The whole group, even chicken man, really seemed to have enjoyed themselves. When it came time to deliver the check, the manager decided to handle it personally and to explain what we had done for them.

"Sir, the dessert board is on us, and of course we did take the chicken and your pasta dish off the bill."

Instead of a thank you and a smile, this particular guest went wild.

"What are you talking about? I told the server that my meal was ruined. The entire check should be on you!"

"I don't understand, sir. Everyone else seemed to have enjoyed their meals. We didn't charge you for the dish that you didn't like, and we sent you a couple of free items, which you also seemed to enjoy."

"You don't *understand*?" he said, with some attitude. "Well what you need to *understand* is that the customer is always right."

That did it. I had to step in.

Now, my staff and I go out of our way to ensure that we are hospitable, but being hospitable never means being subservient or ridiculed. We had done exactly what any other business would have done—replaced a "defective" part with a workable part—and we took it a step or two further. When I approached, the man immediately turned his sights on me.

"How dare you charge me anything for a meal that was ruined!"

"Sir, if I may," I calmly replied. "You sat here for the entire time. You did appear to enjoy everything else, and the rest of your party did as well. We may have misfired on your chicken, and we do apologize for it, but to comp an entire meal just doesn't seem right."

"Well, poor customer service doesn't seem right, either," he said. "You'll be hearing from me."

He begrudgingly paid the check and left. As promised, I received a lengthy email the next day stating that his experience was terrible and that we ruined his night. And although he never touched the chicken, he claimed that he still had the potential of getting sick. And finally, how dare we charge him for a meal he didn't like?

I thought about that for a moment—how dare we charge for a meal that a customer doesn't like? If we operated with that philosophy, we'd be out of business quickly. Not to mention the fact that all the free dishes we comped along our path to the unemployment line would have been eaten anyway. Funny how that works.

Let's consider the opposite situation. What if everybody offered to pay more every time they liked a dish better than expected? Of course, that's not the way the world works. I think most people would agree that this guest overreacted at best, and at worst, they may wonder whether he does this everywhere he goes in hopes of walking away with a fuller stomach *and* a fuller wallet.

I responded to his email. "Sir, from what I understand, you and I agree with everything that happened up until you received your check. You and your party cleaned up every plate we sent out, save the chicken. We apologized profusely for that one dish and provided several others at no cost. So I'm not entirely sure why you feel you should get a full replacement value for everyone's meal."

His reply was short, but none too sweet. "You just don't get it. Customer service is about the customer. You're wrong. Our philosophies toward pleasing a customer are completely different. You should have paid for our entire night, seeing how you ruined it!"

That really bothered me because I have made a living on pleasing the customer. But at this point, there was no winning. This guest was clearly unreasonable and did not deserve further compensation. There was no way I was giving this guy his money back, but at the same time, I couldn't in good conscience keep it. So I sent off a final email.

"Sir, I don't want to take your money. However, I also don't feel it is right to reward your unreasonable complaint. So I've remitted the entire amount of your check to a wonderful charity, the Alex's Lemonade Stand Foundation for Childhood Cancer."

I smiled a little bit when I sent the note, knowing only a monster would reply and demand to receive the money back instead of letting it go to its new destination. To his credit, he did not reply.

And at the end of the day, in some way everybody won. He ended up not giving me any money. I ended up not refunding him. And kids with cancer got a little bit of a boost.

Turning Tables

Restaurateurs are just realtors who serve food

IT'S TRUE, SORT OF. Instructors in college hospitality programs often refer to the restaurant business in terms of the real estate business. When viewed this way, a restaurant is one of the most expensive pieces of real estate around: Every seat can be sold twice each night. What a boon! On the other hand, the ability to sell each of those pieces of real estate expires at the end of each night, never to be sold again. What a bust.

That's why we stress the importance of turning tables. I use that phrase frequently throughout this book, and every night at work. Most restaurants will have two-and-a-half to three turns of the room on a typical night of service, and the goal is to turn each seat at each table.

When you look at the bottom line of the restaurant business, turning tables is the number-one factor that determines whether we thrive or merely survive. And if you don't do it enough, you go out of business. It's that simple.

I always say that one of the worst things a guest can do is to show up very late for a reservation because it affects our ability to maximize the number of tables we turn. But it's much worse to not show up at all. That's like agreeing to buy a piece of property, having me take that property off the market permanently while there are still other potential buyers and then never showing up and paying up. When you book a 7 p.m. reservation and then don't show or call to cancel, my ability to sell that prime piece of real estate is gone forever. If you've ever wondered why we double-check your reservation to confirm your intention of keeping it, now you know.

I believe that if guests truly understood this, they wouldn't be so cavalier in their approach to reservations. To paraphrase *Seinfeld*, anyone can *make* a reservation, but the important thing is to *keep* the reservation. Too many people show up for their reservation at whatever time suits them, expect to be seated immediately and then sit for as long as they like, effectively preventing the restaurant from turning their table. It was worse back in the 1990s when it became fashionable to make reservations at multiple restaurants for the same time and then choose at the last minute, typically hanging the rest out to dry. Thankfully, that practice seems to have died out. A recurring problem that hasn't gone away is the guest who calls at the last minute and says, "Hi, um, our reservation is for right now, and it turns out we just couldn't make it. Can you just move our reservation to a different night? Tomorrow is not a problem for us."

Well, it is a problem for us, and it comes down to simple math. In a forty-seat room, that's eighty seats a night or 560 seats a week. So if we move your reservation for four to the next night, and something happens then, too, we're now down to 552 and counting—backwards. While hitting the number 560 is virtually impossible, turning tables efficiently gives us the best chance to come close.

The challenge from a hospitality standpoint is to never let guests know that in addition to creating a wonderful experience, we also have the responsibility to expedite that experience. There's an old expression regarding extended family visits: "Glad to see you come, glad to see you go." In our business, I would alter it slightly: "Glad to see you come, thrilled to see you leave happy."

So how do we do turn your table without you knowing? It certainly does not entail walking up at a certain point and saying, "Time's up. You don't have to go home, but you can't stay here."

The fact is, we start turning your table the moment you're seated. We constantly monitor where each table is in the course of the meal, and whenever things get untracked—and they usually do—we are prepared to make adjustments. You missed your reservation by ten minutes? We'll make it up by clearing your table between each course in one minute rather than four. Needed some extra time to decide on apps and entrées? We'll take your dessert and coffee-service orders at the same time instead of separately. For all the obstacles a guest can throw at us, we've got solutions. One key to enacting solutions without you even knowing there is a problem is to do so casually and confidently.

Another key is teamwork. Each server is in constant contact with the host and expediter so they can work together to manipulate time on the fly. Let's say a table is struggling to decide what to eat and accepts the few extra minutes the server offers. When the server returns, it turns out they still hadn't looked at the menu due to the great conversation (hey, at least they're enjoying themselves). Third try, and only half the table is ready to fully order; but they're all ready to order appetizers and suggest that they'll order each new course after they finish the last.

That line is the kiss of death for a server; he knows the rest of their stay is going to be a hustle. But he also knows others have his back. He can't appropriately step up to the table to take entrée orders while the guests are eating their first course, so the entrées won't be cooking in the meantime as they normally would. But let's say the server heard one of the guests mention the rib dish (which takes twenty-two minutes to fire) during the aborted entrée order earlier. He may go to the expediter and say, "Table Five is ordering course by course, and I really think one of them is going to order the ribs." On a busy night, the expediter may take a calculated risk and have the cook start on an order of ribs.

When a table is on such a slow pace that running over time is inevitable, the server will alert the host so she can start working on solutions to seat upcoming reservations quickly at other tables, whether it's turning two deuces into a four top, or making a deuce and a four top out of a six. I encourage anybody to study the host at work on any given Saturday night at any restaurant. This careful manipulation of tables is truly an art form.

Nothing ever goes as planned, but we plan for that. One trick is that we do not seat the whole room at once to start the night. If you really wanted to sabotage a night's service, you would fill all 135 seats at 6:00 p.m. Not only would the servers fail to reach 90 percent of the guests within the requisite two minutes, but the kitchen couldn't possibly put out all 135 dinners at the exact same time, not to mention the next 135 after the turn.

So it always makes me chuckle when guests arrive to a half-full room and ask why I can't seat them just yet. I can only tell them to trust me; it's all part of the plan. When we seat tables in fifteen-minute increments, a few at a time, we are able to serve them much more efficiently and hospitably. It keeps the servers sane, it keeps the food hot and it keeps tables turning at just the right pace. It also makes your hour and fifteen minutes feel like just the right amount of time.

Eight Things Guests May Not Know—But Should

Size matters, we don't make the laws and the plate costs more than the food

THERE'S A PLAN.

Most restaurants map out the night, so this four top and that deuce in the first seating may be scheduled to become a six top in the next turn. If a host tells you that the empty table you're pointing at isn't available, they are not trying to be difficult; they're really just trying to keep the flow of service going.

WE KNOW.

Now more than ever, we use today's technology to take notes about all our guests and save them in a database. Special requests, allergies, likes, dislikes, table preferences, ordering trends and even cancellations and reservation modifications are all in there. Information is key in guest service, so let us get to know you. It will make your experience better.

SIZE MATTERS.

Showing up with fewer or more guests in your party than your reservation called for may not seem like a big deal to you. Saying "We'll just squeeze together" may sound as if you're being accommodating, but it doesn't take into account the comfort of the guests around you. Likewise, showing up with two instead of four means there are now two empty (non-paying) seats. The plan in number 1 had you with four; if we had you at two, we could've seated that deuce on the waitlist earlier and shortened their wait. The moment you know your reservation number is changing, just call us. Even thirty extra minutes to rework the plan helps a great deal.

THE PLATE COSTS MORE THAN JUST THE FOOD.

Much more goes into the price of your meal than the sum of the ingredients. There's the obvious labor cost, but what about credit card fees, rent, utilities and of course, profit? Before you complain about the price of your meal, think about what it really cost to deliver it to you.

MUCH GOES INTO YOUR WINE CHOICE—FEEL FREE TO APPRECIATE IT.

I've often heard the debate: "Should I tip for wine service? After all, they just carried the bottle to my table." Not much of a debate to me. Who procured the wine? Who thoughtfully considered many factors and determined that it was the right bottle for your dinner? Who made sure it was stored properly and served well? A professional with hard-won expertise did. Don't leave 'em hanging.

WE DON'T MAKE THE LAWS.

This may come as a surprise to some, but many guests think it's okay to allow their underage children to order alcohol. I get it; when they are nineteen it's pretty close, so feel free in the confines of your own home. However, on our licensed premises you put us in jeopardy of losing our liquor license, the server in jeopardy of losing their job and worse, you create the possibility of a liability claim that could shut our doors for good. Don't pull out the "It's my kid and I said it's okay" card, because "It's my livelihood and the government said it isn't okay." Sneaking them a drink doesn't fly, either.

THIS ISN'T HOLLYWOOD.

It makes for great TV to see the chef spit on the food of a guest who wanted it a little more well done, or to have the maître d' stand with his hand out while you request a new table assignment. That may have happened somewhere at some point, but in a real hospitality environment? Not a chance. Feel free to ask for food exactly how you want it, tell us your likes and dislikes and yes, tip the maître d'—at the appropriate time. Tips aren't bribes and the maître d' who acts like they are should be out of a job.

PART EIGHT

COME AGAIN

*I also knew I would have to have
a talk with the one server still
on staff whose name kept
coming up in a negative light.*

One More Cup of Coffee

We only get one chance to make a final impression

SOMETIMES IT'S THE LAST act of a meal that lingers longest in a guest's memory. So it had better be a damn good one.

Many restaurants seem to consider coffee an afterthought. Sure, they'll ask if you want it, bring it out and maybe even drop the check a moment after setting down the cream. They won't even clear the table after dessert. The feeling is that they've already gotten most of the money they're going to get from you, so they'd rather forego that final $3.50 and turn your table quicker than treat coffee service as a valued part of the meal. But in so many ways, they're missing the point.

In our restaurants, we think of coffee service as perhaps the most valuable $3.50 of your check. It completes the meal, and without it, we run the risk of having you score us with an incomplete grade. Marc will have none of that. Given all his daily responsibilities, you'd be surprised how much care he puts into ensuring that our coffee service matches the quality of everything else on the menu. He spends time sourcing the best beans and exploring new options that purveyors have to offer. Each of our restaurants is outfitted with top-of-the-line equipment, including antique espresso machines from the Italian company Faema, which Marc has carefully restored to their original grandeur and expert operation. He gives such weight to the entire process that no employee may make coffee without him personally vetting their abilities first! To Marc, coffee is much more than a cup of caffeine. It must be the Italian in him.

In Italy, coffee is an art form. It's no coincidence that so many words associated with coffee—latte, espresso, cappuccino—are Italian, and its importance at the end of a meal there cannot be underestimated. Whereas many restaurants in the States serve coffee and dessert together, the Italian way is to serve dessert first and then coffee on its own at the very end. Some Italians will pay their check after dessert and move the party to a café where they know that coffee is taken seriously and will be prepared to perfection. So the onus is on the restaurant to be better than perfect.

We employ the Italian method in our restaurants, with coffee as its own course, even though sometimes we might be better off hurrying through it to get the next group seated. But we resist that urge. Now is not the time to rest on our laurels; it's the time to pull out all stops. So we clear the table completely—not a grain of salt or any superfluous silverware in sight. We cover any spills on the tablecloth with napkin overlays. Every step is part of the overall experience, and it's the foolish restaurateur who does not make that connection.

Coffee service can actually make up for earlier miscues. If we forgot a plate, took too long bringing out a course or missed on a dish, a great cup of coffee during the most relaxing part of the meal can miraculously smooth things over. Maybe we even bring out a gratis glass of grappa with your final beverage. Or I'll sit down and share a brandy with you, or just linger for a moment of conversation, adding to the sense of comfort as you wind down. It's the bottom of the ninth, two outs, bases loaded, full count and we're down a run. Are we gonna look at strike three, or take our best cut and knock it out of the park?

Sometimes coffee is more than just coffee, and it's always worth more than the few bucks it costs. Compared to dating, it's no less important than the kiss good-bye. When done right, you are setting yourself up for another. But a bad last impression could deep-six any opportunity for future romance. It's why we give coffee the importance that we do. If we can leave you fully satisfied, we know there's a great chance we'll be serving you another cup of coffee soon.

Speaking of Gratuities

Is that how little respect you have for the hospitality industry?

ONE OF THE UNIQUE things about dining out in America is the gratuity at the end of the meal. In the rest of the world, service staff are paid a market-based salary or hourly wage, tipping is nonexistent or negligible and menu prices reflect this difference. In this country, there are no other transactions where your main contact's total compensation depends on your good will. Just think about that: How would you like your family's income to rely on other people abiding by the honor system?

I recently watched a cable news roundtable discussion about the future of the gratuity system in America. The panel featured four talking heads—none of whom were currently in the restaurant business—with two in favor of the status quo and two suggesting the tipping system should be done away with. The commentary ranged from surprising to enraging. But before I get to the details, you need to know the basics of the system if you don't already.

Most restaurants pay servers a below-minimum-wage hourly rate. This is legal because the government assumes servers earn most of their money in tips, and servers are bound to include them on their income tax returns. From the restaurant's standpoint, we save money on employee salaries and pass those savings on to guests in lower prices. Some restaurants do add an automatic gratuity, usually eighteen percent, for large groups of eight or more. Otherwise, guests have the option of adding a tip to their bill, and the majority do so. The loose standard is 20 percent, though some always give a little more, others a little less and some use a sliding percentage based on the level of service they feel they've received. Then there are those who decide to tip nothing—or worse, next to nothing—for various trumped-up reasons.

"You know, we had to wait fifteen minutes for a table. It's too bad, but that will affect the tip."

"The wine was so expensive, let's just take it off the tip."

"The food could have been hotter. We'll show them. No tip."

"Sixteen bucks for tax? Screw that, we're taking it out of the tip."

Notice one commonality between those reasons? The server had nothing to do with it. And ironically, it's the people who stiff servers on their tip who usually make the servers work the hardest.

Tip distribution among staff varies from one restaurant to the next, but usually falls into one of two categories. In most places, each server keeps the tips left on their own tables, cutting out a small percent—chosen by them—for bussers and food runners. In many mid-casual to fine dining locations, tips are pooled and distributed with equal shares for servers, plus lesser equal shares for bussers and runners.

When we first opened Vetri, since it was only eight tables and the entire front of house staff (all three of them) worked the entire room, they just shared all tips. As the Vetri Family expanded to seven locations—each of them with more employees and tables than the first—we kept the tip pooling method in place. For one, it was what we knew. But there were also more practical reasons.

It's easier for management to encourage teamwork when every table is the responsibility of every server. It was also clear to every server that luck of the draw was too random to make a nonpooling system work. On any given night, one server could get several six-tops of business people ordering magnums of wine and tipping large amounts, while another would get some deuces and a few family four tops with nondrinkers. Both would serve their tables equally well, but one would earn far less in tips for the same amount of work. Since the latter could happen to every server on any given night, there was a consensus to just share.

A professional staff doesn't need an incentive either way. They help each other out when necessary because they understand that when one is successful, we're all successful. There are also plenty of occasions where someone on staff who never shares in the tipping pool—like the host, manager and sommelier—directly serves a table because their input is needed in the heat of the moment, and their motivation is still the same.

Tip pooling ensures consistency, too. If a server waited on a guest one night and provided phenomenal service, when that guest returns, odds are they will not have the same server but they will still have the same expectation of service. I can confidently say that most of my colleagues who use the tip pooling system provide this consistency as well.

While tipping in general is not often discussed in the industry, a national debate on minimum wage has gotten the nonrestaurant world talking about it all. I suppose it's always a good thing to see the restaurant industry in the news, but I would have been better off missing that cable news roundtable discussion.

The first gentleman who spoke, an attorney, was adamant that the status quo is the only system that will work. His opinion is not necessarily wrong, but his reasoning was brutal.

"If I'm at a restaurant and the gratuity is included, then I know for certain the staff has no incentive to work very hard. I waited tables in college"—which, of course, makes him an expert—"and I know that on nights when I busted my hump I made more money. Simple as that. If I got paid the same amount no matter what, then why should I work any harder?"

Huh? Is that how little respect you have for the hospitality industry? Or maybe it shows how much respect you have for your own job. If I'd been on the panel, I would have asked this so-called expert, "So, if I engage you for your services and you charge me a flat fee, does that mean I get your minimum effort?"

I wasn't any more impressed by the duo who argued that we ought to abandon tipping and pay servers like any other job. Their opinion is also not necessarily wrong, but again, the reasoning was idiotic.

"Restaurant workers all live paycheck to paycheck and their bosses are just raking in money because they don't pay anybody. The owners shouldn't rely on their customers to pay their staff."

Talk about taking the dignity out of what we do, not to mention having a clear misunderstanding of business. Restaurant P&Ls are modeled on the assumption that servers earn most of their income via tips. If the model changed, restaurants would simply adjust the budget to ensure that we paid all our expenses and still—wait for it—made a profit.

Let's say we did abandon the tipping model. I would simply raise our prices by the tipping standard of twenty percent, maintain the rate at which my front of house staff gets paid and create a neutral effect (with the exception of sales tax) on what my guests spend. A $24 dish would now be close to $29, but the tip removed would be almost $5. So the system can be shifted with very little effect on owners, servers or guests.

None of the points by either side added any worthwhile insight. But all the panelists delivered the same regrettable message that there still exists this subtle but pervasive condescension toward the American hospitality industry—and *that's* the thing that has to change!

The tipping system has been around forever and I don't get involved in the politics of it. I will simply implement any policy that benefits all involved and that the government deems legal. Tipping, nontipping, to me they're the same—I honestly don't know which system is better. But I do know this: In the past year alone, the Vetri Family has seen five babies born into the fold, three weddings and six home purchases—all the fruits of hard work by dedicated professionals.

The restaurant industry is a noble one and provides great opportunity, whether you're in it for the dynamic environment, to get on track to a management career or you aspire to ownership one day. No matter where they are or where they're going, every server deserves the same respect as a professional in any other industry.

Comment Cards

Online feedback and playing the Yelp card

ONE OF MY FAVORITE stories from my pre-Vetri days is kind of bittersweet. Bitter because a guy lost his job, which is never good. Sweet because it confirms a valuable lesson for any business owner, and also, I suppose, because I got the guy's job.

The position was manager of a dining room. I was told that my predecessor was relieved of his duties for nonperformance, whatever that meant. It didn't take long to figure out. First day on the job, I set my briefcase down, started placing office supplies in my new desk and in the bottom drawer found thousands of comment cards. It was clear that none had ever been read, for they were as crisp as the day they'd been bound by rubber bands and tossed into the drawer. My first thought was, "Gee, if that last guy had only bothered to look through these, maybe he could have saved his job—and improved the experience of the guests."

I started to thumb through the cards. They covered everything from "food's too salty" to "long time between courses," plus a handful of positive reviews. Some cards included the guest's address, as if they hoped to receive a response, which clearly never happened. I started sorting out cards that fit a trend and soon realized a couple of dishes had received the same criticism multiple times, and one particular server had been called out for his bad performance by several guests. I checked the employee chart and saw that the server was still on staff. I noticed names of servers whose performance had often been praised; none of them were on the chart. I approached the assistant manager.

"What's the process for comment cards?" I asked.

"The guests get them inside the check presenter at the end of their meal, and if they fill them out, their server gives their cards to the manager."

"And then what happens?"

"Well, I really don't know. I suppose the manager would put them in a file or something."

I shook my head. "Well, did he or anyone else respond to the comments? Some guests took the time to write down their address."

"I wouldn't know," he said. "I've never read any of them and the previous manager never really talked about them. Why do you ask?"

"Have you heard of these servers?" I asked, and named the ones whose reviews were all positive.

"Oh yes—great servers. They're no longer with us, though."

"I noticed that. Why'd they leave?"

He didn't know. But I thought I did. They had probably been disheartened by lack of response to comments about bad dishes and bad servers, figured the unchecked negativity would affect them and decided to seek employment at another restaurant where management actually nurtured guests, staff and the back of the house.

I also knew I'd have to have a talk with the server still on staff whose name kept coming up in a negative light.

If you solicit guest comments, you have to act on them. It's frustrating to see a restaurant with the tools to succeed that just doesn't use them. It's hard enough to be successful when you don't have an advantage. One of the greatest tools in the restaurant business is guest feedback, and when it's given in a constructive manner and used to make productive tweaks, it's amazing how much success you can generate without spending a dime on marketing.

Criticism is not a bad thing. We encourage guest feedback and often initiate the process. Many nights after service I will go to Open Table and look through the guests who'd just been in. Often I'll send out six or seven emails to thank them for their visits and ask for specific feedback in return. We also receive unsolicited emails from guests who've eaten at our seven restaurants. Thankfully, very few are negative, but when they are, either Marc or I will reply directly, and always within twenty-four hours.

As far as actual comment cards go, we've replaced those in our restaurants with a more direct approach—soliciting feedback from our guests immediately after their meal by the host staff as they approach the door. On the rare occasion, a guest will stop and say, "Well, since you asked…" and add a complaint or opinion. Whatever the nature of it, the host will immediately call a manager over. The majority of the time the answer is very positive, probably for one of three reasons.

First, I'm confident that our staff was able to recognize any misstep on the spot and quickly turn it into a positive, and by the end of the meal the misstep is long forgotten, replaced by positive feelings. The second reason is that we generally do get it right every step of the way, and our guests are actually happy when we say goodbye. The third thing is that many guests don't like to be bothered, nor do they like to bother us; if they did have a small complaint or concern, they may just keep it to themselves and say to us, "Everything was great" and not really mean it. I imagine their attitude is, "What do they care? They already have my money so I just won't come back," or, "They won't do anything about it anyway, so why bother?"

For Vetri restaurants as well as most of our colleagues', those preconceptions are simply untrue. Without feedback, we're left wondering, "Whatever happened to that guest who used to come in regularly?" Or "Hmmm… those people started off happy, but when they left, they didn't seem so thrilled. They just said, 'Good,' and left. I'm starting to think it might not have been so good for them…"

By the time we realize that something was wrong, it may have happened again and again, and before we know it we have a trend. Once the horse is out of the barn, it's hard to coax him back in. Better to close the door early. And to do so, we need to hear every problem and opinion.

One area of feedback I'd rather do without is online reviews and comments, especially the anonymous variety. My problem is that they are unproductive and often seem to have an ulterior motive. Any comment that doesn't give us a chance to fix the perceived infraction is pretty useless. But I suspect that venting is all these people want to accomplish anyway. I'm not sure what the proliferation of online complaint boards says about our society, but it can't be positive.Another way to garner feedback, which we haven't used yet but have considered, is going to the pros. Some of our colleagues use secret shoppers who come in with an agenda and gather useful information. The idea is that their agents arrive at the restaurant in the guise of regular guests, experience the meal as anyone would and then prepare a report for management. The shopper is given a list of standards and steps of service employed by that restaurant, such as:

1. Were you seated on time?
2. How long did you wait to be greeted?
3. Did you get what you ordered?
4. Hot food hot, cold food cold?
5. Knowledge of the staff
6. Cleanliness of the restaurant

Actual questions are more personalized than these samples, and colleagues have told me the info gleaned is invaluable. We've never taken this step at Vetri because we have always run our restaurants with a very close eye and hands-on presence. My partners and I visit each of them most nights, seeing and hearing for ourselves. Our management team has been in place for a very long time; not only are they our eyes and ears but they've also helped develop our standards and are therefore the best to monitor them. I believe we have the best service staff around. We've created a culture of completely open communication—the only way to success—and our staff have all bought in. They don't hesitate to discuss negative situations—even those they may have caused. On any given night, I may walk into one of our restaurants, have a server notice me and call me over.

"Hey Jeff, I'm trying but I can't seem to connect with Table Twelve. I don't think they like the table, but we're full and I can't move them. Do you think you could talk to them?"

"Of course—thanks for telling me."

They also regale me with the positives, like, "Jeff, Table Sixty-Two was asking for you," or, "I waited on Seven at a previous restaurant and remembered that they love Barolo, so I suggested the new one you just got. Total home run!"

It's all a collaboration, but the most important link in the chain is feedback from the guests.

Food Critics

Everyone's a critic, but just a few are pros

A POPULAR MANHATTAN restaurant group was reviewed not long ago by *New York* magazine critic Adam Platt. While he had good things to say about their first effort, his commentary on their second restaurant was a negative one-star review. The group opened a third restaurant to critical acclaim, but it had not yet been reviewed by Platt. One night he went with a friend for the first of several planned anonymous visits to gather information for his review. He and his friend were having cocktails and a few small plates when a bouncer arrived and told them to leave. Perplexed, Platt asked why, but received no explanation as they were ushered out the door.

Clearly his cover had been blown and the owners, still angry over the negative review, decided they didn't want him there. So Platt took to the internet to tell his tale. I had just finished reading his post when my phone rang for a prearranged interview with *Philadelphia Inquirer* food critic Craig LaBan. I started the conversation before he could.

"Hey, how do you feel about what happened to Adam Platt?"

"What happened?" he asked, somewhat concerned.

"Oh, not like that," I said and proceeded to relate the story I had just read.

He listened intently, and then replied, "Oh, that's awesome." I could almost hear him smile.

"Why awesome?"

"Because it proves that what we do is still relevant to you guys."

Professional restaurant critics at the top of their game in major cities are household names in our industry. We are always waiting for the next Frank Bruni or Pete Wells review in the *New York Times* or Adam Platt's in *New York* magazine. Alan Richman's work in *Bon Appetit* and *GQ* has made him the country's most decorated food writer. Craig LaBan in Philadelphia has people hanging on his every bite and Michael Bauer is known for his insightful reporting on the Bay Area food scene. Tom Sietsema's annual Fall Dining Guide is one of the most anticipated features in the *Washington Post*, and Ruth Riechl's work over the last three decades at the *LA Times*, the *New York Times* and *Gourmet* magazine was highly anticipated.

Established food critics have always been and will always be relevant to us. Early in a restaurateur's or chef's career, it is imperative to strive for a stellar review from an established critic and, believe me, a less than stellar one can have devastating effects. As your reputation grows—in no small part due to positive reviews—one single negative article shouldn't move the needle business-wise one way or the other. Yet established chefs and restaurateurs usually still hope for positive reviews, lest they read, "He *was* great, but all the accolades went to his head and this new effort is awful." Not to mention the fact that we should strive for excellence every single day, review or not, critic or regular guest.

Beyond their impact on the restaurant industry, professional food critics are perhaps more relevant than ever to their readers in today's internet age. The bloggers, Yelpsters, message board trolls and voices in the Twitterverse will come and go, and sensible people will always question the veracity—not to mention the motivation—of their reviews. Not so with the pros.

I'm sure the legit critics must lament the reach of the unchecked internet even more than I do. The old expression "Everyone's a critic" has always been valid, but today every hack with a laptop has a real opportunity to be heard far and wide, not just in their small circle where their groundless opinions can't do much damage. I can only imagine how real reviewers feel when they see that yet another John Doe has launched a food blog with a post about the hot new restaurant that just opened last night, waxing poetic about the experience without interviewing the owner, manager or chef; without giving the restaurant an opportunity to work out the kinks over a couple of weeks; without seeking information on the evolution of the dishes or the story behind the restaurant and its partners; without knowing anything, really, besides the single ninety-minute experience they had on opening night.

It all smacks of a complete disregard for journalistic integrity, but bloggers live by a different code—there's stiff competition to be the first to post a review, complete with lots of iPhone pics. There are a few viable food blogs out there, but most of them operate this way.

Professionals, on the other hand, have actual standards and practices to uphold. The amount of work they put in to turn out a typical-length restaurant review is impressive. I'm not saying this to gain favor with anyone, I'm just telling it like it is. I have great admiration for anyone who works hard to reach a level of professionalism in any field, and I'm always interested in their work ethic and process.

Before they ever strike a key on their computer, a professional critic will visit the restaurant at least two or three times, and rarely during the first week after opening; like any business, a restaurant needs time to get on its feet, hence the familiar term "soft opening." A reputable critic will interview the owners and chef, logging hours of phone calls and research. They ask questions about the inspiration and concept of the restaurant, food-prep methods and innovations, ingredient sourcing, cooking techniques and back-of-house systems, as well as a host of other questions based on the specific restaurant. It's a lot more thorough than the average reader likely assumes.

And then there's us, the front of the house. Anything a professional critic writes about the atmosphere and service, as well as the food, is the result of multiple visits to the restaurant, anonymous whenever possible. While they want to be treated like any other guest, a savvy critic will also test us, quizzing their server about a particular dish. When servers reply with generic comments like, "Oh, the brined chicken is really great," or worse, "Let me go ask the kitchen," it's going to show up in the review.

Of course it all comes down to the food—the focus of most restaurant reviews, and the main thing people want to read about. When you've poured your heart into the restaurant's concept and style, traveled and tested and confirmed a killer menu, hired the best chefs and sous chefs and line cooks, filled the kitchen with the best equipment and then committed as a team to serve every dish to every guest with the standard of perfection, all elements should come together to win you that great review.

It's interesting to see how different restaurants deal with food critics. In many cases, you just don't know they're there since most of them work hard to be unobtrusive. The ones who announce themselves, or who expect special treatment in any way, forfeit all credibility. But most at least try to keep it on the down low. They'll bring friends who make the reservation in their own names and pay the check with their credit cards. They'll come in off the street without a reservation and see if they can get seated. Few critics went to the lengths that Ruth Reichl, then at the *New York Times*, did throughout her career; her hilarious efforts to remain anonymous by donning all kinds of disguises are chronicled in her book *Garlic and Sapphires*. Once success as a critic is achieved, though, anonymity becomes more difficult—just ask Adam Platt.

When the restaurant does know a critic is present, their real attitude toward critics emerges. Some take a laissez-faire position: "I don't care what he writes. I'm confident in what and how we serve every guest, and besides, we are already busy." For them, the critic is simply a mandatory thing that happens within two months of opening and, regardless of what the critic writes, they know their restaurant will do well because it's a destination in a popular area, or they're capitalizing on a hot trend, or the chef's name alone commands attention.

Then there's the opposite take: "Oh no! A server noticed that the reviewer from the *Times* is here! Let's stop everything, hit the reset button, trash the mise en place for new ingredients and focus solely on that table right now." This attitude is rife with problems. Mainly, it's not worth it to disregard everyone else to service one table. Potentially pissing off 150 guests to please one? I hate those odds. But it happens. I know one local restaurant operator who literally trashes the ingredients that have been prepped and starts all over with brand new ingredients when he hears that a critic has entered the restaurant. Not only is this impractical, but more importantly, if your mise en place isn't good enough for the critic, what about the rest of the customers who've been eating there?

When we know a critic has arrived at Vetri, we don't do anything differently than on a regular night. I'd be lying if I didn't say the mood among staff doesn't change the moment we hear of their presence. It's human nature to be a little nervous when you're being graded on something. But we're prepared, since our general philosophy is to treat each guest as if they are an anonymous and important food critic. When you operate from that point of view every night, you don't have to change a thing.

One night a woman came in who identified herself as a high-ranking member of a reputable food organization who would be sharing her experience with her group. She had an air about her that suggested she was fishing for special treatment. She didn't ask for a comped meal, but what she said to the manager afterward did the job just as well.

"I noticed that a few of the regular guests sitting near me had ordered the same dishes that I had."

"Yes they did, and we're glad that you were able to experience some of our most popular dishes," the server replied.

"That's not what I meant. What I meant was that I sort of expected to get a little extra, maybe a special version of those dishes, being that I am here representing my popular food organization."

How do you answer something like that? Simple: you don't.

One night, during our third year in business at Vetri, a gentleman came in out of the rain near the end of service, alone, and asked me, "Any chance you'll still let me get dinner?"

"Of course," I said and seated him at a deuce.

Peeking out the kitchen door on one of his many nightly status checks, Marc noticed the guy seated alone, did a double take, then called me over and said, "I think that might be Alan Richman from *GQ*. I ran into him a few months ago and he mentioned he gets back to Philly occasionally and might swing by."

"That's cool," I said, and then got back to work. But it really was cool.

Richman, professional that he is, wrote nothing after that first visit. Over the next few months he stopped by for dinner periodically and finally announced he was writing a piece about Vetri. National press was rare for us at that point. Little did we know the impact his article would have, starting with its title: "Is This the Best Italian Restaurant in America?" More than a decade later, people still come in quoting lines from that article.

Contrast Alan Richman's comportment with that of another well-known food writer who visited the restaurant early on (and who will remain nameless here). Even before his arrival, we kind of knew it was going to be a disaster. We'd been informed of certain requirements up front that set off red flags, the most egregious of which was his assertion that no check was to be presented—he expected to be comped.

He arrived thirty minutes late, looking harried. In the middle of my description of the specials and wine options, he stopped me.

"Here is what we want," he said abruptly. He pulled a pen out of his jacket, opened the menu and literally circled all the dishes he wanted.

In the face of such rudeness, I responded in as professional a tone as I could muster.

"Certainly. Is there any particular order you would like to see this all in?"

With a dismissive wave, he replied, "You bring it out in an order that makes sense."

I went to the kitchen tell all this to Marc, who nearly flipped when he saw the marked-up menu. Things just went downhill from there.

It quickly became clear that this guy had come to our restaurant not wanting to like it. He spoke and gestured with a mocking air throughout the evening, at one point even dramatically fanning out his shirt as if to say we got the room temperature wrong. This in the middle of summer in a packed room during the peak of service.

Midway through dinner, he announced, "I have a train to catch. Can we speed this up? Just bring all the food at once."

When I informed Marc, he refused. "I'm plating the pasta now. He ordered the whole fish and the steak, which I am sending out as their own course. Sending them with pasta makes absolutely no sense."

I agreed; I couldn't imagine a situation where a seasoned restaurant writer would want to mix the two courses, either. So we served the pasta as a separate course. And we heard about it.

"I wanted it all together!" he exclaimed.

"Yes, sir, but when you requested that, Marc was already plating your pasta. Also, the fish and steak are set as their own course, naturally."

He chuckled, looked at his table mates and said to them, "Chef can't even get the dishes out when the guest wants them."

With that statement, it hit me. This man had built a name for himself over the years but had fallen victim to his own ego. He believed he was bigger than the work he was doing and had decided that *he* was the show. His guests were simply there to witness, not to share a great meal. When the disaster was over and he stood up to leave—without so much as an attempt at his wallet—we said goodbye and wished him well.

Marc was disappointed that a national restaurant critic would treat us this way and wasn't content to just let it go. He wrote the guy a letter and invited him to come back when he has time to experience a complete Vetri meal, not when he wanted to play "Ready, Set, Eat."

The national critic's response to Marc's letter was even worse than his behavior during the meal. He actually typed three single-spaced pages ripping into pretty much everything we did while enumerating all the meals he'd had recently that were so much better. At the time, we were worried because we were still relatively new and understood his influence in the food world. Luckily, he didn't waste too much ink on us. We continued to grow and, truth be told, his star doesn't shine today as brightly as it once did.

Once in a while Marc and I laugh at the fact that we are still standing despite his prediction of our demise and that the only press he's received in the last few years has been negative, addressing his unprofessional policy of accepting—or is it demanding?—freebies.

Afterword

WHENEVER I MEET people who are curious about the restaurant business, they ask how I handle the long, hard hours. I counter with the old adage, "Find a job you love and you'll never have to work a day in your life."

Regardless of their profession, I don't know any successful people who aren't "always working." I love the hospitality industry and have since the day I first punched the time clock at a catering company when I was a teenager. If I had found another calling in life, I would have worked just as hard to be successful.

But no job is as hard as being a father. Nothing is as important as consistently setting a good example for my children. I believe that they understand a healthy work ethic and hope that we show that to them daily. But sometimes I wonder if they really get it, and I wonder how a conversation might go if the topic were raised at the dinner table.

"Dad, what would you do if I didn't get an A in school?"

"I'd ask if you tried as hard as you could and gave it your best effort."

"What if I did and I still didn't get an A?"

"Then I would be proud of you for trying so hard, and I would help you set goals to do better next time."

"So I wouldn't get in trouble?"

"Of course not. There are two instances where you can get in trouble with me for school performance. One is if you don't do your best; and you just said you did your best, so you're safe there."

"What's the other?"

"If you stop being nice to others. I can stand just about anything, but if the principal called to tell me my daughter wasn't a good person, that would probably be the worst thing I could think of."

I have the same theory with my extended family—the Vetri Family—and I look at the whole group as my kids, in a sense. How do you get kids to act in a manner you would choose for them? Set an example.

Very early in our partnership, Marc and I made a commitment to each other that if we were to become profitable, we would also become philanthropic. We are, after all, in the service industry, and if we had the means, we should serve the community at large as well as the guests in our dining room. At first, we figured that we would simply give to charity in the form of distributing restaurant gift cards to be used in auctions that raise money for good causes, picking the nonprofit organizations that did work that was close to our hearts.

Soon after we opened, we realized we had reached a position that would allow us to start the process, and we started offering gift cards for auctions as planned. But soon, a member of one of the organizations we partnered with said, "Of course I'd like you to donate to our charity, but I'm happy to hear when someone does something beyond donations—anything, really—to further the cause."

So in 2004, I cold-called the director of a foundation called Alex's Lemonade Stand. Founded in 2000 by a four-year-old cancer patient named Alex Scott, it was already having an impact on funding research into pediatric cancer cures. Unfortunately, Alex passed away in 2004 at the age of eight. Her parents continued her work and have established a world-class foundation that has generated over $80 million, relying heavily on people who erect makeshift lemonade stands and donate their proceeds. Just before making the call, I had participated in a charity event that, among others, brought together several accomplished chefs to donate their services, feeding all involved with fantastic foods. Brilliant!

During my call with the founder's mom, Liz Scott, I asked for a meeting and she agreed. I pitched her on the idea of reaching out to my colleagues in the hospitality industry and asking if they would do an event similar to the one I'd recently attended, but for Alex's

Lemonade Stand. I conceded that she didn't know me or our abilities in the charity realm, so I asked if she would allow me to hold a couple of small events and show her what we were capable of. She agreed, and we got to work.

As it was January, the month Alex was born, we decided to hold a birthday celebration in her honor, and we raised $2,000 that night. We followed that up with a larger event that brought together five of our local colleagues in the Philadelphia restaurant scene, and that effort brought in close to $30,000. We decided to kick it up a notch, and invited chefs from around the country, so that in addition to raising a lot more money, we would increase awareness. We had just opened Osteria and were happy to offer that space free of charge; all the chefs we contacted were excited to get involved and everyone's participation helped us reach by far our highest total at that time, nearly $250,000.

The following year, in typical Philly style, it was go big or go home. We got the city to close Broad Street—the biggest street in Center City—right in front of the restaurant. We doubled chef participation as well as revenue. By now, we were fairly confident that we had credibility with Liz and her organization. When we informed her of our increasing revenue projections, she expressed concern that if we turned over operations to the Foundation, it might be too risky for them to lay out so much up-front money without any guarantee of return—she explained that it's hard for a nonprofit to spend money in order to make money, and we understood. So I asked her what would happen if I spent all the money and simply cut them a check from the proceeds. Her concern with that option was that if people wrote their checks to us, the Foundation wouldn't get the tax break associated with the donation. So... how could we combat that?

In 2008, we established our own 501(c)3 organization, the Vetri Foundation for Children. Originally we assumed this foundation would simply subsidize the philanthropic habit we had developed. But it has grown so much since then.

Anyone who has started a nonprofit knows there's a lot more to it than simply saying, "Hey, let's do some good." As we quickly learned, in addition to the forms and regulations necessary to register as such, we needed to form a board of directors. Taking our social responsibility seriously, we sought out the people we thought could best give us direction. At the very first meeting, this group of nine business leaders from Philadelphia posed a simple question: "We admire the work you're doing around pediatric cancer research, but why aren't you focusing on an issue where you can make a change for the better in an area you know intimately?"

"What issue is that?" we asked.

"The global crises of obesity and food insecurity."

That did it. We do know food, and we'd figured out how to market it for a profit; perhaps we could use that knowledge to help provide nourishment to people in underserved communities. That initial conversation led to the Vetri Foundation program called Eatiquette, which makes the connection between healthy eating and healthy living. It continues to grow, enabling local schools to provide nourishing food that is locally sourced, freshly prepared and completely paid for by us. It encourages family participation and stable social environment. We aren't reinventing the wheel, only trying to reintroduce it. This is the way families have eaten for generations, and we want to help make that connection again.

Hunger affects us as a society, regardless of social class or geographic location. One out of every three children risks developing type 2 diabetes, and sadly, the current generation of kids is the first that risks not outliving their parents. From an economic standpoint, this global health issue will affect all industries' ability to hire and retain quality employees, and it will drain our national healthcare costs. Not to mention that it is inhumane to sit idle while our neighbors suffer.

The glaring difference between this fight to feed people and that of pediatric cancer is that we are fighting to find a cure for pediatric cancer, while we already know the cure for hunger. We just need people to accept it.

Why does this make a difference to an independent restaurateur? In addition to the good reasons outlined above, the main reason we do what we do is much larger than being successful businesspeople. I'm a citizen of the world, and even more importantly, I am a parent. I want to see my kids flourish in an environment that is vibrant and full of opportunity. What we do, how we make a living, that will likely end with us. However, the way we live will continue long after we are gone.

So I encourage you to get involved, do something, do anything to make tomorrow brighter for everybody.

Acknowledgments

I GET TO do what I do every day because of the love and support I get at home from my wife, Melissa, and our daughters Rebecca and Ali. They serve as constant reminders of what is truly important.

My mom Annette, sisters Suzy and Rissa and their families have always been unbelievably supportive, trekking to Philadelphia every time we open a new place and enduring my opening-night jitters.

My father, of blessed memory, always told such great stories and I think he'd get a kick out of the fact that I shared some with you. Thanks also to my in-laws, the Lelchuks and Schusters, for understanding the hours of a restaurant and allowing me to be the family hospitality consultant.

Marc Vetri is far more than the ideal partner; he is literally the brother I never had. Marc and his entire family took me in when I moved to the City of Brotherly Love, and made it just that to me.

Jeff Michaud, Brad Spence, Tia McDonald and Adam Leonti comprise the culinary team that continues to reinvent the Vetri Family and keep us relevant. They have such a deep-rooted belief in preserving Italian culture.

Matt, Gina, Jill, Ashley, and Kelsey, the management and staff of the Vetri Management Company keep me sane--I literally couldn't do this without you.

Nancy Benussi jokingly refers to herself as the Vetri Family Mom. I take that seriously. She is the first in and last out of every crisis situation.

Steve Wildy is not just the Jerk Whisperer, he is the Beverage Pimp, Counselor, Educator (for real), a shoulder to cry on and a true friend.

Carolyn Pagnotta embodies what it is to be a member of the Family. Two daughters is plenty, but if I were to have another, I'd want her to be just like Carolyn.

Greg Jones simply "gets it." He translated what I said into readable words that sound like me. Greg can be part of our Family any time.

The entire Vetri Family make me so proud every service. I must single out Erasto Perez, the only remaining member of our opening team with me and Marc. He epitomizes service, loyalty and most important, family.

IN REMEMBRANCE

Sadly, during the writing of this book, the Vetri Family lost a member to cancer. We were blessed to have known Gabriel Mellul. He was the quintessential front-of-house manager who made us laugh every day. His memory will be preserved through the lessons we learned, and all future Vetri Family members will know the name Gabe.

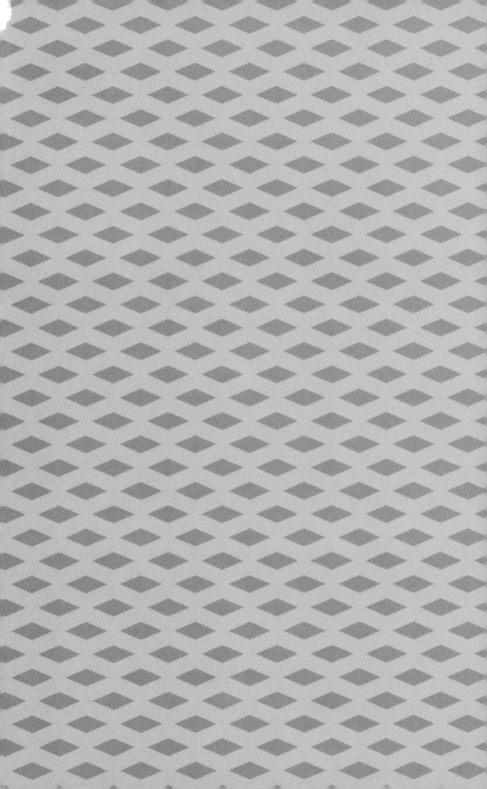

MAIN LIBRARY
361 Washington St
Brookline, MA 02445
4/15